Karin Schumacher / Claudine Calvet / Silke Reimer

The AQR Tool –
Assessment of the Quality of Relationship

Based on developmental psychology

Translated by Gloria Litwin in collaboration with Shirley Salmon

With DVD

zeitpunkt musik
Reichert Verlag 2019

This publication was supported by funding
from the Research Council of Norway (grant number: 240433).

Cover image: marble sculpture *Spiegelung* by Simon P. Schrieber,
with courtesy by the artist.

Bibliographic information published by the Deutsche Nationalbibliothek
The Deutsche Nationalbibliothek lists this publication in the Deutsche Nationalbibliografie;
detailed bibliographic data are available on the Internet at
http://dnb.dnb.de.

Printed on acid-free paper
(resistant to ageing – pH 7, neutral)

Table of Contents

0. Guidelines to the book and DVD

Foreign words and specific technical terms are explained in the glossary at the end of the book. In this book the therapist will be referred to as she and the child as he.

The enclosed DVD illustrates the AQR Tool using film sequences from music therapy. Individual examples can be selected from the menu. As well as the films, this DVD contains the four lists of characteristics of the AQR Tool as PDF files as additional accompanying material. These can be printed and used as work sheets. In order to open these PDF files you need version four of Adobe Reader or higher or another PDF application of your choice. Adobe Reader is available free of charge from the Adobe website (www.get.adobe.com).

1. Introduction

1.1. History of the AQR Tool

The music therapist Karin Schumacher has been working since 1984 with children with severe developmental disorders who are suffering from an impairment in social, interactive and communicative abilities. The work with these children led her to look for the origins of the ability to develop interpersonal relationships. The realization that the ability for organised perception is the basis for all further development of the ability for relationships, and that this "organisation" is missing in children with severe developmental disturbances led to intensive work on prenatal sensory development. In music therapy practice, games with music, movement and speech, which are developed from observing the child, create a so-called "coordinated stimulation" (Schumacher, 2017, 1st edition 1994) and help to integrate the individual sensory impressions. At the same time proprioception has a special significance. Through the child's own body weight, the therapist is able to help the child by means of physical, vocal and musical interventions to experience contact to his own body and to connect sensory perceptions. Based on this, it is to be assumed that rocking and carrying as well as early mother-child games are prerequisites for the development of the ability to develop interpersonal relationships (Schumacher in Decker-Voigt et al. 2009, 1st edition 1996).

In 1990 the collaboration began with the developmental psychologist Claudine Calvet who, in her research, had specialized in aspects of early childhood, especially early interaction disturbances in mother-child relationships in children with trisomy 21 (Down Syndrome) (Rauh, et al. 1999; Rauh & Calvet, 2004; Calvet-Kruppa et al., 2005). Video sequences from Karin Schumacher's music therapeutic work have been systematically analysed by both researchers. Their focus was at first on therapy moments in which progress in the development of the child was evident.

In her publication "Musiktherapie und Säuglingsforschung" (1999) [Music Therapy and Infant Research], Karin Schumacher scrutinizes the self-concept of the infant researcher, Daniel Stern. This led to her looking at the clinical picture of autism from a developmental psychology point of view. Experience from practical music therapy work showed that basic abilities such as meaningful processing of stimuli and the early ability for affect regulation can develop later through music therapy. Through the collaboration with Calvet, this view was complemented by results from attachment research (Bowlby, 1969, 1998; Ainsworth al. 1978) and, later, brain research (Hüther, 2003, 2004).

The AQR Tool was developed over ten years in the search for evidence of the effectivity of music therapy interventions. At first, the handling of music instruments and the child's instrumental expression were focussed on, which led to the development of the scale for instrumental quality of relationship (IQR) (Schumacher, 1999). Examination of vocal pre-speech expression followed, which led to the development of the scale for vocal quality of relationship (VQR) (Schumacher & Calvet-Kruppa, 1999). For the assessment of the ability for relationship in children who could neither express themselves instrumentally nor vocally, the scale for assessment of physical-emotional quality of relationship (PEQR) was developed (Schumacher & Calvet-Kruppa, 2001). The scale for assessment of therapeutic quality of relationship (TQR), which focusses on the therapist and her intervention technique, was developed inn order to assess the child's ability for relationship, also in the context of therapeutic interventions (Schumacher & Calvet-Kuppa, 2005).

A reliability analysis followed for which over 80 raters, experienced colleagues and students from Germany, Austria and Sweden, at first were trained in the application of the assessment scales to assess the presented video sequences using each scale. The agreement with the assessment as well as with each other was illustrated statistically. The reliability of the AQR Tool could therefore be proved (Schumacher, Calvet & Stallmann, 2005).

The DVD "Synchronisation" shows five films with relevant moments of music therapy work with children on the autistic spectrum (Schumacher & Calvet, 2008). Here the focus is on the awareness that synchronous moments especially improve the ability for relationship.

1.2. Latest revision and further development of the AQR Tool

Silke Reimer, an instrumental teacher who received her diploma in music therapy in 1999 at the Berlin University of the Arts (UdK) Berlin, carried out research into "Kurzzeitige Wechsel von Beziehungsqualitäten in der Musiktherapie" (Reimer, 2004) ["Short-term changes in quality of relationships in music therapy"]. In preparing for the publication of the AQR Scales, she analysed the results of the reliability analysis, especially the raters' comments on the scenes that were difficult to assess. These data form the basis of this publication. Supervision and training led to a deeper understanding of frequently asked questions.

The book "The interpersonal world of the infant" (Stern, 1985), upon which the previous work on the AQR Tool is based, was revised in 2000 with a new introduction. This critical revision of selected aspects of the self-concept have practically no influence on the AQR Tool. However, the question is raised of whether the observations and knowledge that form the foundation of the AQR Tool are in line with the latest infant research. This question concerning Stern's self-concept is addressed in the chapter about the developmental psychological basis of the AQR Tool.

1.3. Training

Further training in which the theory-based application of the AQR Tool is taught has been offered since 2005/2006. Thorough training is a prerequisite for qualified application of the AQR Scales as an analysis of video sequences by means of the scales without knowledge of the theoretical foundation and without practising the application frequently leads to a superficial or even incorrect assessment.

In the certification courses offered at the University of the Arts Berlin, for example, the developmental foundations of each of the four scales of the AQR Tool and their practical application are imparted and are practised by assessing video examples. The first module in these courses contains Stern's model of development and the synactive model of neonatal behavioural organization (Als, 1986) as theoretical foundations. A general introduction to the development of the AQR Tool is followed by the TQR Scale with the assessment of video sequences. In the second module, ways of visualising AQR analyses are presented. The main topics are the developmental psychological foundations of emotion regulation and the development of attachment, and the introduction of the PEQR Scale. The participants are asked to bring examples from their own work on each of these topics to practise the application of the scales. The topic of the third module is the development of the vocal pre-speech expression. The main topic of the fourth module is the scale for instrumental expression. Here questions are explored concerning how and when an object, here a musical instrument, can be meaningfully handled, which movement is "easy" and which needs further development. These play a big part not only in the assessment but also in the choice of the therapeutic method. For example, beating and shaking are, from a developmental psychological point of view, earlier movements than holding a mallet and directing it to a sounding instrument and the more sophisticated fine motor skills needed for string playing.

The certification course concludes with an exam. Each participant at first assesses in writing an example from their own work with an analysis of his/her music-therapeutical interventions and then presents this assessment to the other participants using film examples. Participants should describe their experience of using the AQR Tool in their own work. Successful completion of the course confirms that the participant is able to apply the AQR Tool independently and effectively.

The course graduates meet once a year to ensure quality in the application of the AQR Tool and to further developments in the AQR Scales in various fields of indication (see "Zertifikatskurs EBQ-Instrument" at www.udk-berlin.de/musik-therapie). This forum offers opportunities for discussion on relevant topics such as the AQR Tool for diagnostics, for documentation as well as for reviewing intervention techniques. Music therapists from the same field of work come together in networks to exchange ideas over and above the yearly meeting.

1.4. Transference to further fields of application

Various publications in German show attempts to transfer the application of the AQR Tool to other areas (Körber, 2009; Warme in: Muthesius et al., 2010; Salmon, 2010; Reimer, 2010, 2016). Comparison with other German diagnostic tools (OPD-2: Körber, 2009; OPD-KJ: Burghardt-Distl, 2009) had already been suggested in 2005 by Frohne-Hagemann and Pleß-Adamczyk.

It is evident that a one-to-one transference is not meaningful, as the interpretation of physical-emotional phenomena of expression must always be based on the clinical picture and its specific characteristics. In order to transfer the application of the AQR Scales to other areas, the clinical characteristics of physical-emotional, vocal pre-speech and instrumental development as well as speech development are at first studied and differentiated. A reliability analysis must take place again whereby trained raters reassess the assessments with the help of numerous video examples. Before publication, it is necessary to consult the authors of this book in order to protect the AQR Tool from superficial use and to ensure it is applied in a reliable way.

2. Developmental psychology basis

2.1. Daniel N. Stern's model of development

In the book "Musiktherapie und Säuglingsforschung" (Schumacher, 1999/2004), insights into the emotional and interpersonal experience of infants are connected with contact and relationship disturbances in children with pervasive developmental disturbances.

The fundamental questions here are:
- Which developmental steps does an infant pass through before he interacts with his caregiver as a partner in dialogue and play?
- What hinders this development in children with pervasive developmental disturbances?
- How can differences in development and behaviour be observed and assessed?
- Which music therapeutic interventions help to positively influence the symptoms and/or support the next steps in development?

Schumacher (2004, 1st edition 1999) initially describes Stern's layered model of development (Stern, 1985). Starting from this theoretical basis, she considers the symptoms in children with pervasive developmental disturbances, especially children on the autistic spectrum, and emphasizes the insights which lead to a better understanding of the contact and relationship disturbance of these children.

In this chapter, the procedure underlying the development of the AQR Tool is concisely presented. The revised version of the book: "The interpersonal world of the infant" (Stern, 2000) is used, whereby Stern critically considers selected aspects of the model of development in the introduction. The terms of the AQR Tool correspond to the revised edition of the assessment scales.

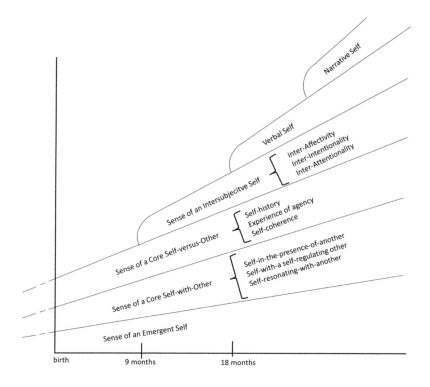

fig. 1: Layered model of delevopment (by Stern 2000) adapted for music therapy

Sense of an Emergent Self

According to Stern, the ability for amodal perception and for cross-modal transfer is innate. The connection and integration of sensory perceptions is associated with appropriate emotional perceptions. This is the prerequisite for a meaningful perception of the environment and the increasing ability to create "order". Stern describes the perception of an emerging organisation as an "emergent self" (Stern, 1985). In his revision, Stern expands this definition. He describes a so-called "present moment" (Stern, 2000, S. xviii) in which the infant senses himself as the "living vital experiencer" (ibid). "The intentional object is whatever the mind is stretching toward" (ibid). An infant with these abilities for perception and emotional experience is able from birth to make eye contact and to imitate human behaviour. The infant's experience is accompanied by so-called "vitality affects". With this term, Stern describes "a quality of experience that can arise directly from encounters with people" (Stern, 2000, p. 54). Stern expands his discussion by mentioning the findings of the infant researcher A. R. Damasio, and describes the so-called "background feelings" as follows: "All of these body signals come from the self –

an as-yet-unspecified self. Such signals need not be attended to. They need not enter into awareness. Yet they are there in the background. They are the continuous music of being alive." (Stern, 2000, p. xviii). According to this, vitality affects are changes and modulation of this "music". The being and experience of the infant is determined by these background feelings (Damasio, 1999, p. 286) and vitality affects.

Children with pervasive developmental disturbances, especially children on the autistic spectrum, appear not to have, or to have only an incomplete ability for connecting perceptions. They are not able to integrate the incoming stimuli so that they can process them meaningfully. Presumably, and this is even more crucial, they are also unable to process these stimuli in a way that could lead to a change or modulation of the background feelings. If sensory impressions are not adequately connected to background feelings, a severe "experience disturbance" can be assumed. Vitality affects therefore arise either not obviously or so delayed that they are not registered by caregivers as emotional reactions. Therefore, we experience a child as "difficult to read" in his state of affect. From the point of view of the child, this "experience disturbance" could also be a reason why eye contact is not sought. Additionaly, the ability for imitation, together with vitality affects and the ability for eye contact, which Stern sees as the third characteristic of the emergent self, is not adequately developed.

In music therapy, we consider these children to be "contactless" and avoiding. At first, they react neither to the therapist nor to the sound of music or musical instruments. They neither express themselves vocally nor instrumentally and stay imprisoned in stereotyped behaviour.

In the AQR Scales, this behaviour is described as modus 0: "lack of contact/ contact rejection". Here interventions are helpful that accept the child in his momentary state and at first create an "enveloping atmosphere" for the child. Basing his interventions on the child's own body weight, the therapist can help to effect a connection of sensory perception. Carrying and rocking must therefore be dependent on the child's own body weight. A coordinated "stimulating atmosphere" evolves from the child's movements being made audible in an exactly attuned rhythmical way. The experience: "I hear what I feel" (perhaps also "… what I see") leads to an "emergent experience" (Stern, 2000, p. 52), which means the experience of a self-organizing perception. A short reaction, such as a glance toward the source of sound, can result from successful intermodal connection. This is modus 1: "contact-reaction".

Sense of a Core Self

The sense of a core self has, just as the emergent self, its origin in prenatal time. In comparison to the original model (Stern, 1985), the sense of a core self is divided into two layers: The sense of a "Core Self-versus-Other" and the sense of a "Core Self-with-Other".

From the music therapeutic point of view, we begin here with the sense of a core self-with-other. Stern formulates in this context three sub-categories:

- *Self-with-a-self-regulating-other*: In order to develop a coherent sense of physical self as basis for the experience of agency, the infant must be regulated in his affect by others.
- *Self-resonating-with-another:* According to Stern, here the sense of core self finds itself in a partial "overlapping" with another.
- *Self-in-the-presence-of-another*: Here Stern means the physical and psychological presence of another, whom the infant perceives as a "framing environment" (Stern, 2000, S. xxiii). This psychological presence enables the infant to remain psychologically alone with himself.

In children with pervasive developmental disorders, especially children on the autistic spectrum, affect dysregulation can be seen. The inability to really perceive another leads to the child lacking experience in being resonant and/or in feeling the presence of another. Using intervention techniques, the music therapist first helps to regulate and shape the child's state of affect. The therapist uses instruments to give resonance and, becoming affectively involved, accompanies the child's so-state. However, the therapist does not intervene in the child's actions unless they are destructive (see section on over- and understimulation).

The sense of a core self becomes possible through experiences that the infant makes as invariants in a changing environment. These are:

- *Experience of agency:* The infant experiences himself as agent of his actions. This involves the intention to perform a specific action, the experience that he can control his actions, and the expectation of specific results from this action.
- *Self-coherence:* the infant senses his body as a whole and experiences it as separated from the body of another.
- *Self-history:* The infant experiences the ability to change while staying the same person. This also involves the sense of affects that remain the same in these experiences, independent of the original situation (cf. Stern, 2000, p. 90).

Children with pervasive developmental disturbances, especially children on the autistic spectrum, frequently lack the experience of initiating actions themselves and experiencing a desired result. The chances of experiencing authorship can also be "missed" if too much is taken over by the carer. Passivity and lack of exploration can be the result.

A further characteristic of a disturbed sense of authorship might be the controlling and functionalizing of situations and people, which is often accompanied by high tension (see modus 2 "functionalizing contact").

A lack of self-coherence is often the reason for a lack of ability for exploration and playing. An attempt is made to compensate the lack of self-coherence through stereotyped action, resulting in a lack of self-continuity. Music therapeutic interventions here should enable the experience of agency. The child experiences self-efficacy by the therapist supporting the child's intentional actions, making him aware of them, and not demanding any form of dialogue. These interventions lead to the experiences required for the development of self-awareness described above (modus 3).

Sense of an Intersubjective Self

Between the 7th and 9th month infants become aware that they can share their own subjective experiences with other people. The child is capable of being aware of the emotional state of another person and of connecting this to its own emotions. In this way, intersubjectivity is possible. Stern describes three characteristics which help to mark the onset of intersubjective relatedness (Stern, 2000, p. 128):

- *Sharing joint attention (inter-attentionality):* Infant and mother direct their attention jointly towards an object. However, the infant then returns his gaze to the mother in order to "read" in her face if joint attention has been achieved.
- *Sharing intentions (inter-intentionality):* The infant gives the mother "signals" that communicate the infant's specific intention to her. The infant can experience a mutual understanding of intention and motivation.
- *Sharing affective states (interaffectivity):* Stern names social referencing as a special characteristic. The infant "reads" the emotional states of the mother through eye contact and attributes this as meaningful for his own feelings, especially in insecure situations. The infant "somehow makes a match between the feeling state as experienced within and as seen 'on' or 'in' another" (ibid., p. 132).

In children on the autistic spectrum seen as having pervasive developmental disturbances, the characteristics which Stern describes as significant for intersubjectivity are absent at first. Eye contact is disturbed and the ability to recognize emotions in oneself and in others is absent. Therefore no affective exchange can take place.

In order for the child to have awareness of the other and to come to an intersubjective experience, all of the steps of development described above must first of all take place: the development of an emergent self, the development of the sense of a core self versus other and in the presence of other. As Stern puts it, "(…) the possibility of sharing subjective experiences has no meaning unless it is a transaction that occurs against the surety of a physically distinct and separate self and other" (ibid., p. 125).

In children with pervasive developmental disturbances, the layers described above cannot at first be observed. Only when the child can be regulated effectively and can show interest in the outside world, can the therapist appear as person. If the child directs his attention jointly with the therapist to a third party or object, then the first signs of intersubectivity are evident. Glances to the therapist with the desire to find his own experience confirmed in the therapist show the ability for social referencing (modus 4). For the first time the therapist feels involved as person. She can now present herself and her interventions more and more as a person with her own ideas. If the child begins to attune to the therapist's playing and reacts to changes in her playing, interactive playing can develop in which both players bring in and exchange motifs equally. This modus is called "interactivity" (modus 5).

For "interaffectivity" (modus 6), Stern's advice is important for the music therapeutic work: the infant, at an earlier point of his life, has felt jointly experienced inner states; only later do joint states arise which refer to something outside of this dyad. For this reason we also speak of "affect attunement" in modus 2. Here, however, the therapist starts exclusively from the child, while the interaffectivity of modus 6 means reciprocally attuned and mutually influencing states of emotion. The ability to play in the sense of purposeless joint playing with musical means are connected to positive emotional experience. Shared pleasure and fun are observable here and leave unforgettable marks in the experience and therefore in the brain of the players.

2.2. Early organisation of behaviour

In addition to Daniel Stern's self-development concept, insights into attachment and infant research (Bowlby, 1951; Ainsworth, 1974, 1978; Bowlby, 1979; Main et al., 1985; Crittenden, 1996, 2000; Fonagy, 2001; Ziegenhain, 2001; Grossmann & Grossmann, 2004) have been presented in the previous work of Schumacher and Calvet (1999, 2001, 2004, 2005, 2007, 2008).

The research focusses on the ability to enter into and create an interpersonal relationship, as well as the role of the relationship for emotional development, here especially affect regulation. Thus, these insights are also relevant for the evaluation of the ability for relationships by means of the AQR Tool.

In the following sections, the importance of behavioural organisation (Als, 1986) for the AQR Tool is considered and complemented through brain research (Hüther, 2003, 2004).

Behavioural organisation as basis for eye contact and interpersonal exchange

According to the model of neonatal behavioural organisation of the infant (Als, 1986), the infant is equipped with a homeostatic equilibrium principle (Brazelton, 1973), which means he attempts to keep his inner state in balance. To reach this balance, he has four basal adaptive behavioural systems at his disposition that enable him to regulate himself.

These behavioural systems develop prenatally, beginning with the physiological system, then the motor system, etc. and are present at birth. In order to communicate emotionally and socially, it is necessary that the first three systems are in a balanced state. The physiological system must be brought into a state of inner calm,

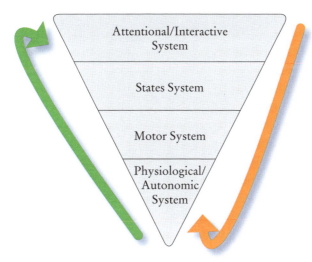

fig. 2: Model of the synactive organisation of behaviour development (Als et. al. 1982)

and a sleep and wake rhythm must be found. The result of this developmental step is a state of attention that is the necessary basis for every interaction. This organisation remains of lifelong importance and constitutes a development model.

If an infant becomes unbalanced through internal or external influences, we speak of a "stress model". Recognising signs of stress that indicate unregulated systems is especially relevant for therapeutic work. An extensive presentation of stress signs can be found in Derksen (Derksen & Lohmann, 2009). If a therapist is able to recognize and understand these signs, she can intervene appropriately and neither overstimulate nor understimulate the child. The systems named above will be described from the perspective of infant research, and their importance for music therapeutic work will be illustrated by means of examples.

Prenatal sensory development

The next figure shows the order in which the senses develop prenatally. As each sensory perception is presumably connected before birth with sensations, this connection between perception and feeling also plays a central role after birth.

fig. 3: Prenatal sensory development

	touch, feel 	taste 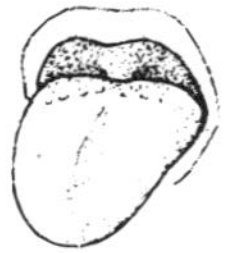	smell 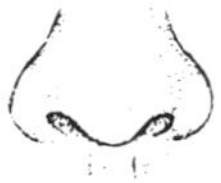	balance 	hearing 	seeing 
before birth						
end of 1 month		laid out				
2 months	area around the mouth reacts sensitively to stimuli		olfactory epithelium differentiated			
3 months	hand, oral cavity and body surface generally stimulus and pain sensitive			labyrinth laid out, can already perceive stimuli; vestibular systems begin to function	cochlea constructed	
4 months		mature			further differentiation	
5 months						rod cells differentiated
6 months	vibration, pain, pressure, temperature are felt by the hand (end of 6th month)			maturation		
7 months			maturation		all structures mature	
8 months		reactions to discomfort			reactions to external sound stimuli	
9 months						reception of light stimuli complete

As mentioned before, all these perceptive experiences are connected with emotional experience that also needs to be integrated.

The interactive system

After birth the infant is still dependent on these processes of sensory coordination associated with emotional experiences. Only when perception and sensation are brought into attunement can primary awareness develop. Background feelings (Damasio, 1994, p. 286) can be mobilised, especially in interpersonal relationships. Through contact with the caregiver, special emotions develop that only arise in interpersonal space. These feelings, which Stern calls "vitality affects", are especially stimulating for the baby and need therefore to be regulated, particularly in the first six months, with the help of the caregiver. Normally this occurs through body and eye contact and the voice. If this affective regulation is successful, the infant's interactive system becomes stabilised. In this system of interaction, he expresses his emotional state through the voice (babbling, sounding, squeaking, sighing and crying) as well as mimicking (searching for eye contact, eye contact, looking away, making grimaces, staring).

As the infant is born with an especially fine sense of "intensity" behind which the emotions are concealed, we will focus on this topic here. The following question arises: how strong or weak should stimuli be so that they can be processed by the infant? During the first year of life the infant sorts the stimuli according to the questions: Do I know the intensity of this stimulus or not? Can I integrate this stimulus, or does it overwhelm me? Is it pleasant or not?

The special importance of pauses

In an optimal situation in which an adult relates to the infant with either a calm or happy voice, with facial expression as well as with adequate distance, new-born babies search for eye contact and experience someone reacting positively to them. The infant stays in eye contact with his caregiver until he can no longer process what he has experienced. Then he turns away and makes a so-called "pause" (Papousek et al., 2004). The pause is necessary in order to integrate the perceptive connections as well as the emotions that arise. Thus, what has happened can be sorted and integrated into cognitive higher structures. In this case, the competences up to now are efficient, and the infant experiences over time that he can optimally regulate himself. These "good organisers" (Rauh et al., 1994) are more resistant to stress, more robust, have a better physiological regulation, acquire good abilities for self-regulation and can ultimately also calm themselves. The focus is on the stability of the behavioural organisation and on the openness for social stimuli. Children who have a good regulation system become emotionally well-balanced. They can integrate new stimuli better and keep this balance.

For the therapist's methodological approach, the use of pauses is crucial; these can appear in various ways. If integration of sensory impressions is possible through the intervention of the therapist (modus 1), the child experiences an affect which leads to a contact-reaction. Now it is the task of the therapist to lead her intervention to a close, to allow a pause, and in this way to enable the child to process this experience.

> **Example**: Florian jumps up and down on the trampoline. At first the therapist follows Florian's stereotyped hand movements, and then supports his desire for movement. This strong "being moved" is accompanied by a melody and leads to a perceptive connection of hearing and sensing (proprioceptive) stimuli. Florian reacts for a short time with a smile. The therapist leads the intervention to a close, whereby a pause occurs (see DVD, PEQR modus 1).

From the point of view of the child, pauses in AQR Scales are described in modus 4. Here the child makes a pause on his own initiative, can end this pause on his own initiative and return to contact. He uses the pause for self-regulation. However, the therapist always makes pauses where her intervention should be processed by the child.

> **Example**: Tanja presses the therapist's hands, and the therapist integrates this offer of contact into a push-and-pull game. Tanja explores her own hands, and through eye contact looks for confirmation of her physical experience. She begins to regulate herself and her emotional state through pauses and glances to the therapist and to the camera person (see DVD, PEQR modus 4).

The system of sleep and waking states

All systems of behavioural organisations are closely linked to each other. In this way, the interactive ability is greatly dependent on the degree of wakefulness and the guiding and sustaining of attention. On the side of the ascending development model, the degree of attention and wakefulness shows the level of responsiveness of the infant and his ability to relate to his environment. If the infant is unbalanced, this state shows itself in newly born babies through crying or even falling asleep; later transitions such as whining or dozing can also be observed.

For the therapeutic approach, it is important not to immediately direct the aim of intervention at the interaction, otherwise the child could be overstimulated and his stress level could increase. If, in music therapy, the child shows kinds of behaviour such as crying or screaming, interventions should be appropriate in order to help regulate his high affect (see also TQR modus 2).

> **Example**: The therapist must dedicate herself totally to the child's high affect and tension. She improvises a song that makes affect attunement and affect shaping audible and tangible (see DVD, TQR modus 2).

The motor system

If stimuli cannot be integrated, an inner tension arises, and, according to the descending model, the motor system becomes activated. If the infant is stabilised within this system and makes pauses, his movements are related to his body and focus on its centre. For example, putting the hands together or touching one's own body are signs of this kind of self-regulation.

If balance is not achieved through self-regulation, the infant shows that his inner tension is rising through motoric signs of stress. These signs give information about the degree of stress, for instance, muscle tone (taut or flaccid), the tempo of a movement (slow, hectic, frozen), or the kind of movement (fist, spreading fingers, overstretching the head, arching the back). Other clear signs of stress are turning away and avoidance. In this case, the infant's inner state can only be regulated with outside help.

In music therapy, we can see not only signs of regulation and stress but also kinds of behaviour that indicate an unregulated motor system: stereotyped behaviour such as rocking, jumping, compulsively walking around, etc. These can be indications that primarily the motor system needs to be regulated before the child can become calm and attentive. Therefore the therapist will direct her interventions at first to the child's physicality.

> **Example**: Ludwig frequently handles a piece of string in a stereotyped way, repeatedly showing strong body tension. Being swung in a hammock, accompanied by the therapist's singing, leads at first to a sense of his own body whereby he does not need the stereotyped behaviour any longer.

The system of physiological reactions

If the strong excitement continues, signs of physiological stress are increasingly evident. Examples of this are: a raised pulse; skin reactions (pale, marbled or patchy); breathing reactions (irregular, strained or forced, hiccups, retching and spitting). These and other signs of stress, divided into light, middle or severe, give information about a person's subjective experience of stress, and can arise throughout the person's life in stress situations.

As becomes evident in the examples mentioned above, it is crucial for the child's development to avoid over- or understimulation and to react in a sensitive way to the child's behaviour as outlined below.

Sensitivity

According to Ainsworth (1974, 1978), sensitivity is characterized by the following attributes: the caregiver is attentive and is aware of the infant's signals; she correctly interprets these signals and reacts promptly and appropriately to the infant's behaviour. If this kind of sensitive caring person is available for the infant (Calvet-Kruppa, 2001), the pauses needed for the infant during the interaction are not interpreted as rejection. The caregiver waits calmly and attentively until the infant himself returns to the relationship through his gaze.

Overstimulation/understimulation

If the caregiver does not understand the meaning of the pauses, she may become insecure or even feel rejected. In a pause, the infant protects himself from further stimulation, whereby he shows no readiness to search for the gaze until he has processed what he has experienced. If the caregiver insists, and looks for eye contact, changes the position of the child's body, kisses, tickles and puts the infant under pressure, the child experiences overstimulation. The infant is overloaded, remains in avoidance, the system topples, and stress signals arise in all systems. This leads to difficulties in recovering balance, as a destabilisation in one area has an immediate influence on another. In this way, stimuli are experienced as overload and their processing is not possible.

If the overstimulation lasts for weeks or months, the duration of the infant's avoidance increases, and finally leads to defence. This becomes chronic and leads to emotional instability and a reduced ability to organise himself in a stress situation. In such cases, the infants mainly have negative emotional experiences with their caregivers. Frequently this results in a real "passing each other by", whereby the caregiver seeks contact while the infant has turned away. However, if the infant is ready to come into interaction again, the caregiver is possibly no longer available, stays distant and shows no reaction to the infant's search for contact.

In the end, massive inadequate actions by an adult can cause the system to collapse. Here the child "freezes". This freezing has the function of stopping a massive release of cortisol, which can have an immediate influence on various organs and on the organisation in the brain (Hüther, 2003).

Particularly in children with a disability, the focus is on the behavioural organisation, as many systems are not as mature and/or well-organised as in "normal" new-born babies. The adult's intuitive and affective attention is even more crucial for further development. Frequently it is the excessively high intensity and complexity of a stimulus, of being too fast, that will lead to avoidance, as the stimuli cannot be integrated. The resulting lack of positive emotional experience in exchange with the caregiver leads to a disturbance in the relationship.

All these processes which happen in the social interaction can also be seen early on in the physiology. The expectation of a reaction from the caregiver is already developed in two-month-old children: their heart beat slows down. Through other social experiences, for example, imitation, it becomes faster (Trevarthen, 1998).

Insights from brain research

In his work, Hüther describes how the ability for relationship can continually influence the malleable brain. Only the experience of supportive caregivers can help the child to develop the experience of self-coherence (Hüther, 2005). "Giving support" here primarily means the consistent physical experience of being carried, being cradled, and being rocked.

The film "In search of shared time" (Schumacher & Calvet, 2008) shows that synchronous moments can produce this self-coherence. Hüther supports these findings in his article about levels of salutogenetic effects of music on the brain (Hüther, 2004). Hüther emphasizes that, through hearing music found to be pleasant, through active playful music-making and through free singing, a harmonisation and synchronization of the generated neural activity patterns in the various regions of the brain can be achieved. These effects are likely to be even more distinctive the more pleasant the musical experience is subjectively judged, the more open the person in question is to this experience, and the extent to which the person is able to admit free associations (to dream) (Hüther, 2004, p. 20).

We now know that, especially in a pervasive developmental disturbance, affective harmonisation is the prime focus, as associative thinking presumably cannot develop without this. For this reason, the observation and assessment tool AQR (Assessment of the Quality of Relationship) focusses especially on the emotional processes that accompany a relationship.

2.3. Developmental psychological and brain physiological basics of the preverbal period

Based on the work of developmental psychologists such as Trevarthen and Stern, the development of the infant without disabilities is described. In **table 1** the AQR scale referred to is indicated as follows:

Red = Physical-Emotional Qualitiy of Relationship (PEQR)
Blue = Vocal / Pre-Speech Quality of Relationship (VQR)
Orange = Instrumental Quality of Relationship (IQR)

Unmarked passages refer to general aspects of development.

Age to 12 months	Developmental psychology	Brain organic maturity
Pre-birth		All senses are already present (see fig. 3, p. 20).
		Awareness of sounds and music begins.
		Synaptic growth activates the pre-frontal areas of the brain in which self-regulation will later happen.
		Through the multisensory quality of music, the brain can connect synapses.
		The fourth foetal month until the end of the third month of life: first phase of myelinisation (sheathing and/or insulating layer) of the auditory pathway (pre-thalamic part).
		Myelinisation of certain nerve fibres leads to speedy transfer of impulses (from 2 m/s to 50 m/s).
		Only in the course of development does myelinisation of nerve strands take place in the brain. Myelin "cements" learned and retained ways of behaviour.
		5th or 6th month pre-birth: nerve cells of the inner ear are able to function and react primarily to middle levels of frequency.
	Foetus freezes in awareness of verbal disputes (Hüther)	From the 6th month: extra-uterine acoustic stimuli are perceived.

Age to 12 months	Developmental psychology	Brain organic maturity
0–0.1		Birth: Weight of brain: 350 gr. Till 3rd year of life: tripling of weight. Brain is primarily very "malleable". Primary task: guiding of functions and behaviour to adjust to the environment. Experiences structure the brain, the most important of which are relationship experiences. Touch, smell, taste, sense of balance, hearing are developed (see fig. 3, p. 20).
		Brain maturity results through basal experience of togetherness, contact and pauses.
		When the caregiver sings, this stabilizes and modulates the tension level of the infant, especially when connected to movement (cradle song). Verifiable through cortisol levels.
	Formation of primary communication processes or primary inter-subjectivity (Trevarthen).	Phenomenon of mirror neurons explains learning through imitation: the same neuronal pattern is activated through observation of movements and activities.
	From birth, the newborn baby can see and imitate (Meltzoff).	

Age to 12 months	Developmental psychology	Brain organic maturity
0–0.1		

The left temporal lobe of the cerebral cortex reacts to speech. Mirror neurons fire not only through observable activities, but also through acoustic stimuli.

Sight and hearing are coordinated.

Visual perception is organised.

Vision capacity: Newborn babies have keen vision at 25 cm and perceive strong contrasts.

Supramodal perception: differences in rhythm, intensity, and form are perceived from birth (Stern).

Eye lens: Nerve connections are completely developed.

Optic nerve: Myelinisation is still incomplete at birth.

Following of objects is possible in a saccadic (jerking) pattern.

Laterally presented stimuli lead preferably to an orientation reaction.

Age to 12 months	Developmental psychology	Brain organic maturity
0.1–0.4	Regulation and stabilisation of physiology through caregivers. Formation of inner calm and attention as basis for successful emotional exchange (Als).	
	6 to 8 weeks: can maintain eye contact (Gibson). Exchange of vitality affects (Stern).	
	8 to 10 weeks: social smiling (Spitz). Beginning communication with others. First recognition of trusted caregiver, first rudimentary expectations.	
	Infants whose parents often answer their vocalisations in the first half year cry less at the end of the first year of life, vocalise more and use gestures as communication (Ainsworth and Bell).	
	8 to 28 weeks: focus of attention on external events, especially everything that moves (mirror neurons).	

Age to 12 months	Developmental psychology	Brain organic maturity
0.1–0.4		Development of visual-motoric skills: from 1 month, open visual orientation reactions, long focussing on objects.
	Pre-syllable state: at 2 months: Basic sounds. 2 to 3 months: beginning of pre-syllabic cooing and exploration sounds (Papousek).	From 2 months: calm following possible, normal orientation reaction, good movement awareness. Between 2 and 4 months: "Synapses spurt" in visual cortex.
		Up to 4 months: strong myelinisation (comparable with adults only from 2 years of age).
		Recognition of melodies that were frequently heard in the two months before birth. Newborns stop crying and become calmer through the music.
	At 3 months: with the development of head control, production of a wider range of vocalisations (group of sounds "eh" (Ä) and RR; R-chain; building of consonants, consonant/vowel groups, sounds with closed lips, "Ah"-sounds, repetitions, laughing, screaming, change of vocal range; proto-conversation: vocal prattle (Herzka)).	Differentiation of rhythmic stimuli-patterns in the form of regular and irregular heartbeats.
		2 to 3 months: myelinisation of the motoric roots of the cranial nerves (V, VII, IX, XII), that participate in the production of vowels.

Age to 12 months	Developmental psychology	Brain organic maturity
0.1–0.4	From 3 months: understanding of mood changes in the sound of the voice and intonation, the beginning of vocal exchange with more sounds in positive mood.	2 months: recognition of consonance and dissonance, recognition of individual out-of-tune sounds, i.e. very slight differences of pitch in microtonal range are perceived.
	Objects are grasped through innate gripping reflex and moved to the mouth.	From 3 months: sensibility for pitch and chroma.
	Sight increasingly influences the hand movement (Piaget).	In the 3rd month until the 5th year of life: second phase of the myelinisation of the auditory pathway (thalamocortical projections to the primary cortex).
0.4–0.8	4th to 5th month: first established interaction expectations, caregiver is increasingly recognized as initiator of play.	4th to 6th month: massive growth and refinement of the brain structures (limbic system and cerebral cortex); the cortex increasingly takes control.
	From 6 months: preferred forms of play - play with objects, with the body, with the caregiver.	From 6th month: further building of sensory processes (holding reflexes, balance) and motor skills.
		Further myelinisation of the motoric speech area (Broca's Area).
	5th month: "da" and "ma" sounds.	From 5 months: perception of simple rhythmic changes (long-short vs. short-long).

Age to 12 months	Developmental psychology	Brain organic maturity
0.4–0.8	From 6 months: reaction to the calling of own name.	Pre 6 months: recognition of short variable melodies. Melodic contour is the most important characteristic of differentiation.
	6th to 7th month: beginning of regular babble of syllables; M and V sounds; vowel change; calling sounds and angry calling sounds; refusal sounds; whispering.	From 6 months: differentiation between timbres and larger volume variations, preference of rhythms that are structured according to simple time relation and form principles (regularity, ability to summarize in rhythm).
	8 months: chain formation, recognition of dialogue principle.	
	Hand-eye-coordination is established (Piaget and Butterworth).	Visual perception: from 4.5 months - Differentiation between adjacent objects on the basis of shape variation.
	From 4 months: can follow the direction of the caregiver's gaze (Bruner and d'Entremont).	From 5 to 9 months: use of colour variations.
	4 to 5 months: with increasing development of arm-hand-control comes increasing interest in objects; duration of eye contact to caregiver sinks from 80% to 15% in favour of the object (Bruner).	Between 3 and 6 months: development of visual motor skills - begin of anticipatory eye movement based on the maturation of the projection of the deeper cell layers of the primary visual cortex to the frontal field of vision.
	Up to 6 months: interest in people or objects; no connection to each other (Bruner).	Up to 6 months: the sharpness of vision has improved and reached the quality of vision of an adult. Binocular vision (far and near sight).

Age to 12 months	Developmental psychology	Brain organic maturity
0.4–0.8	5th to 6th month: first aim-directed activity (almost intentional). The caregiver is used as a means to an end, to achieve the aim without being looked at (Bruner).	Summary: there is a connection between the development of the visual motor skills and attention. Improved connection of perception (touching, feeling one's body, hearing and seeing) still remains the focus of early development (see references on over-and understimulation in chapter 2. 2).
0.8–1.0	8 months: secondary intersubjectivity (Trevarthen & Stern). 9 months revolution (Tomasello): beginning of communication with one person over an object, joint attention becomes established. The child can follow the direction of attention of the caregiver (Moore & Dunham). Emotional social referencing is established (Striano & Rochat); exchanges of smiles during play; stranger anxiety (memory) (Spitz); object permanence (Piaget); first simple imitation (Meltzoff).	7 to 9 months: maturation of motoric regions of the brain, maturation of sleeping and waking centres. Connection between the halves of the brain.

Age to 12 months	Developmental psychology	Brain organic maturity
0.8–1.0	From 9 months: separation of syllables (da-da; ma-ma).	8 to 10 months: infants from Western cultures are able to differentiate between diatonic as well as non-diatonic changes (easier with changes in melody or triad sequences, which correspond to the Western tonal system).
	Around 9 to 12 months: beginning of imitation of sound structures.	
	Need to communicate increases.	
	Up to 12 months: babble monologue (la-ba-ga-ba-ba-ba), sm/b/p/n and vowels.	
	Adult speech is followed attentively; first understanding of words.	
	8 to 10 months: looking; fixing of gaze on near objects. Begins to look at the caregiver at the same time.	
	11 months: understanding for gestures; understands the meaning of pointing. Points to objects that are removed (Bruner).	
	From 8 to 14 months: pinch grip (median: 9 months).	

Age to 12 months	Developmental psychology	Brain organic maturity
At 12 months	Joint attention is connected to positive affect.	By the end of the first year: early infant reflexes are lost.
	Beginning of imitation and learning of vocal structures of the mother tongue (Papousek).	
	End of the first year: the experience that the attention of another can be reached through vocalisation, which means sounds and patterns have a semantic meaning (Bruner).	1 year: highest synapse density in the visual cortex- around a billion synapses per cubic millimetre. Further maturation of the pre-frontal cortex (PFC) with the connection to knowledge (memory).
	First words.	
	Gestures and gaze are used in order to make adults do something for the infant. They steer the adult's attention toward a mutually interesting aim (Butterworth).	

Table 1 is based on the research results of early developmental psychology from the following authors: Ainsworth et al. (1974), 1978; Als (1986); Bruner (1979, 1982); Butterworth (1989, 1998); D'Entremont et al. (1997); Gibson (1979); Meltzoff & Moore (1977); Meltzoff (1988); Moore & Dunham (1995); Papousek (1994, 2001); Piaget (1952, 1954); Spitz (1965); Sroufe (1997); Stern (2000); Striano & Rochat (2000); Tomasello (1993); Trevarthen (1993, 1998).

Information about the development of the brain is based on: Brisch (2008); Gembris (2005); Hüther (2007); Rizzolatti & Sinigaglia (2008); Schmidt & Schuster (2003).

3. The AQR Tool

3.1. Overview with organigram

The AQR Tool focusses on the way relationships to oneself (body and voice), to objects (music instruments) and to others (the music therapist) are developed. With the aid of specific characteristics, the quality of this ability for relationship can be assessed and therefore determined in a comprehensive way. A short version of the four lists of characteristics of the Physical-Emotional Quality of Relationship (PEQR), the Vocal Quality of Relationship (VQR), the Instrumental Quality of Relationship (IQR) and the Therapeutic Quality of Relationship (TQR) has already been published as a method for microanalysis (Schumacher & Calvet, 2007). In the following sections, they have been revised and are presented in full length. As shown in the organigram, each scale contains, firstly, the description of specific focusses of observation. In the four lists of characteristics, the main characteristic of each modus is pointed out, followed by descriptions of each focus of observation. At the end of each scale there is a table with an overview. However, it is recommended at first to use the more detailed lists of characteristics for assessment.

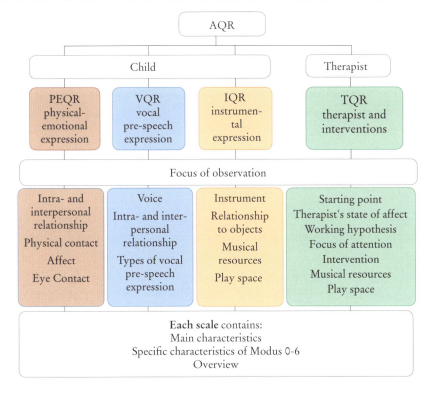

fig. 4: the AQR Tool

3.2. The four scales

PEQR: Physical-Emotional Quality of Relationship

Focus of Observation

1. *Intrapersonal/Interpersonal Relationship*: the development of one's own body awareness and the ability to be in physical contact or exchange with the therapist.
2. *Physical Contact*: the acceptance or desire of the child to be touched, to be held, to be rocked, and to have active physical contact.
3. *Affect*: The affect can be seen in facial expression and physically observable forms of behaviour.
4. *Eye contact*: The quality of the eye contact and the type and duration of eye contact to the therapist are assessed.

Modus 0 Lack of Contact/Contact Refusal

> The main characteristic is the restriction of social interaction. The child is unapproachable – mostly stereotyped behaviour can be observed. The child's emotional expression is difficult to interpret. There is no eye contact.

1. *Relationship*: Self-coherence as in intra-synchronization is not developed. The interpersonal space is not yet open.
2. *Physical Contact*: The child either rejects physical contact or shows no reaction to it.
3. *Affect*: The affect is difficult to interpret. For no obvious reason, it goes quickly from neutral to restless.
4. *Eye Contact*: The child makes no eye contact.

Modus 1 Sensory Contact/Contact-Reaction

> The main characteristic is a passive acceptance of physical contact. If the connection of the coordinated stimuli offered by the therapist is successful, short positive reactions can be observed.

1. *Relationship*: An awareness of one's own body becomes possible through intermodal connection, whereby the proprioceptive perception is crucial as a basis for self-coherence. A fleeting awareness of physical contact can be evident.

2. *Physical Contact*: The child allows physical contact, albeit passively. He allows himself to be physically touched, carried or rocked.
3. *Affect*: If the intermodal connection is successful, the child reacts with a short positive vitality affect.
4. *Eye Contact*: The experience of intermodal connection leads to the beginning of organisation, which in turn leads to vitality affects. The child shows only fleeting, often sweeping glances that are searching for the source of this organising feeling.

Modus 2 Functionalised Contact

> The main characteristic is a high inner tension. The therapist must react to this and allow herself to be functionalized. The child's body and face express high tension and restlessness. The overriding mood is one of tension. The eye contact can contain a controlling aspect. The affect is in the foreground.

1. *Relationship*: The high tension of the child's body indicates a non-coherent body awareness. The therapist places herself at the child's disposal in order to regulate the affects and allows herself to be functionalized.
2. *Physical Contact*: The physical contact is unregulated, i.e. closeness and distance are not balanced. Either the child is overwhelmed by auto-aggression and directs this aggression against his own body or he shows aggression towards someone else.
3. *Affect*: The child experiences that he is threatened or overwhelmed by his own high affect. Significant unrest and exaggerated, distorted, ambivalent facial expression can be observed. The high affect can culminate in auto-aggression or aggression towards another person.
4. *Eye contact*: With auto-aggression the child does not look at the therapist; with external or object aggression, the child's gaze is fixed on the therapist's face, thereby controlling the therapist's reactions.

Modus 3 Contact to Oneself/Self Awareness

> The main characteristic of this modus is the awareness of one's own body as the origin of activity (self-coherence). The child desires physical contact in order to perceive himself in his self-effectiveness and authorship. He appears to be attentive and calm. The child's gaze follows his own movements and actions.

1. *Relationship*: The child can initiate a relationship to himself as in intra-synchronization. The movements stemming from the body centre are coordinated. The child experiences himself hereby as the centre of activity and as author of his movements. This enables contact to himself as the basis of self-coherence. The presence of the therapist enables the long-term exploration of his own body or that of the therapist.
2. *Physical Contact*: Physical contact is now not only accepted by the child, but even desired. He shows this clearly through his posture. In order to be more aware of his own body, he explores and discovers his own body and/or that of the therapist.
3. *Affect*: A calm, clear, attentive state of affect continues.
4. *Eye contact*: The gaze has a quality of calm observation and follows the child's own movements and activity.

Modus 4 Contact to an Other/Intersubjectivity

> The main characteristic is the ability for inter-attentionality (joint attention). The child shows interest in the therapist and in the joint activity. The body is utilized for interpersonal experience. The child includes the therapist in his awareness. The child regulates his own affect through exchange of eye contact and pauses.

1. *Relationship*: The ability for inter-attentionality (joint-attention) develops. Through this, the relationship to the therapist also develops. Mutual desires become possible (inter-intentionality).
2. *Physical Contact*: The physical contact achieves an interpersonal quality. The child's own physical sensations can be confirmed (social referencing) by the therapist.
3. *Affect*: The need to involve the other in his own experience leads to more self-coherence and self-affectivity. The child regulates himself affectively by exchanging eye contact with the therapist and making pauses.
4. *Eye contact*: Joint focus of attention on the musical-physical activity becomes possible. The child seeks eye contact with the therapist when he has experienced something new (social referencing). It can happen that the child looks in the direction of the person who is filming (triangulation of perception).

Modus 5 Relationship to Another/Interactivity

> The main feature is the mutually desired dialogical physical contact. The child enjoys the physical contact. The exchange is relaxed and accompanied by a positive affect. The child regularly exchanges eye contact with the therapist.

1. *Relationship*: Longer continuation of inter-attentionality leads to an intensifying of the relationship. The relationship becomes established and child and therapist react to each other dialogically.
2. *Physical Contact*: The child himself initiates physical contact to the therapist and can also respond to or end it organically (pauses). He enjoys the physical contact.
3. *Affect*: Both partners increasingly find themselves in a positive state of affect (smiling). Longer lasting interaction as in joining in and imitation or question and answer games take place in a positive atmosphere. However, the continuing positive atmosphere must not become too intense.
4. *Eye contact*: The longer lasting intentional interaction of longer duration is evident in frequent exchanges of eye contact.

Modus 6 Joint Experience/Interaffectivity

> The main feature is pleasure. The relationship is firmly established. The body serves playful exchange and can be symbolically expressive. The child can express pleasure and fun. This emotional quality is reflected in the eye contact.

1. *Relationship*: The relationship is secure in the sense of secure attachment. Trust in the reactions of the therapist becomes established. The child and the therapist are able to relate to each other without restriction and to regulate the nearness and distance.
2. *Physical Contact*: The physical contact is playful and role playing can develop. The physical expression can have a symbolic meaning.
3. *Affect*: Body and affect become unified. A continual postive affect develops, which the child copes with and is shared by the therapist (interaffectivity). Authenticity and emotional flexibility become evident.
4. *Eye contact*: The ability to "play" and to have fun is also reflected in the eye contact. This eye contact can transmit high positive affects without threatening the relationship.

tab. 2: Overview of the PEQR characteristics

PEQR	0	1	2	3	4	5	6
Relationship intrapersonal	no self-coherence	body awareness develops	high tone	self-coherence	confirmation of self-coherence through another	appropriate tone	confident acting with own body
Relationship interpersonal	no obvious contact/contact refusal	short awareness of physical contact	functionalizing	self in the presence of another	intersubjectivity	established	confident
Physical contact	none	allows passive physical contact	aggressive	self awareness through physical contact	confirmation of physical experience through another	inter-personal quality	playful
Affect	difficult to interpret	short positive arousal, otherwise neutral	high affect	calm	need to involve another	longterm relaxed and positive	harmonious pleasure and fun
Eye contact	none	fleeting	none (auto- aggression) controlling (aggression to another)	attentive	social referencing with pauses	regular exchange of eye contact	emotionally flexible exchange of eye contact

VQR: Vocal Pre-Speech Quality of Relationship

> Focus of Observation

1. *Voice*: general assessment according to duration and form of vocal pre-speech expression in a music therapy context with regard to the quality of relationship.
2. *Relationship*: intrapersonal: Vocal expression gives the body proprioceptive feedback whereby a relationship to one's own voice develops. Interpersonal: vocal expressions in an interpersonal context are assessed. The foundation is formed by developmental psychology research into the way one's own vocal expression is discovered during the course of development, how it is played with, and how it enables an interpersonal relationship.
3. *Types of vocal pre-speech expression*: description of types of vocalisation in their quality of relationship.

Modus 0 Lack of Contact/Contact Refusal

> The main characteristic is a lack of vocal expression.

1. *Voice*: There seems to be either no awareness of vocal offers from the therapist, or they are not inviting. The child shows no vocal expression or vocal reaction.
2. *Relationship*: No relationship can be observed either intra- or interpersonally.
3. *Types of vocal pre-speech expression*: No types of vocal pre-speech expression can be observed.

Modus 1 Sensory Contact/Contact-Reaction

> The main characteristics are brief vocalisations that are an expression of inner emotion.

1. *Voice*: Being moved physically in the sense of intermodal connection leads to intra-synchronous sensations and stimulates vocal expressions. The vocalisations are the result of inner emotions. This experience often results in a glance towards the source of sound. Vocal expression, mostly as vocalisations of pleasure, are audible as an expression of vitality affects.
2. *Relationship*: Vocal expressions give proprioceptive feedback, whereby an intrapersonal relationship develops between the child's voice and body. There is probably no awareness of these vocalisations as coming from oneself.

3. *Types of vocal pre-speech expression*: Basic vocal sounds and noises are expressed without prosody. Vowel-like sounds can be observed. Vocal expressions of pleasure have more resonance and show more modulation.

Modus 2 Functionalizing Contact

> The main characteristics are vocal expressions which are the expression of a high affect in the sense of inner tension.

1. *Voice*: The voice is used to express internal distress. It is used as an expression of one's own desperate needs. Vocal expression can also appear in a less urgent manner in a stereotyped way.
2. *Relationship*: An intrapersonal relationship (voice and body of the child are clearly correlated) and a functionalized interpersonal relationship can be observed.
3. *Types of vocal pre-speech expression*: The vocal expressions display vowel-like sounds that have, however, no modulation, are strained and lacking in resonance. Sound, pitch, rhythm and dynamics display no variations (stereotype); the expression is connected to the high affect. High emotional intensity can lead to corresponding volume of the vocal expressions. No form develops.

Modus 3 Contact to Oneself/Self Awareness

> The main characteristic is the sense of authorship and explorative way of using one's own voice.

1. *Voice*: There is an awareness and exploration of one's own vocal expressions.
2. *Relationship*: The intrapersonal relationship becomes evident. The child's body receives proprioceptive feedback from the vocal expression. The audible result is recognized by the child himself as his own production (authorship), whereby his vocal expressions are of longer duration.
3. *Types of vocal pre-speech expression*: The vocal expressions range from breathing sounds to vowel-like sounds that are modulated through listening to himself. Sound, pitch, rhythm and dynamics are explored and varied. A form develops through therapeutic intervention.

Modus 4 Contact to Another/Intersubjectivity

> The main characteristic is awareness of the therapist through joint vocalisation. The child's desire is to find confirmation of the experience of his vocal expressions in the therapist (social referencing).

1. *Voice*: There is a need for social referencing of the experience of vocal expressions.
2. *Relationship*: The interpersonal relationship becomes evident through the desire for social referencing. Inter-attentionality is achieved through a shared focus of vocal expressions. The desire for togetherness becomes evident (inter-intentionality).
3. *Types of vocal pre-speech expression*: The vocal expressions lead to vowel-consonant connections that can be linked to gestures. Synchronous moments are endured for a longer period. Sound, pitch, rhythm and dynamics are attuned. A form develops through the conscious awareness of beginning, pause and end. The vocal utterance is activated through positive confirmation from the therapist and thereby gains in expression.

Modus 5 Relationship to Another/Interactivity

> The main characteristic is the developed ability to imitate. In the dialogical exchange of motifs, mutual referencing as well as the keeping of pauses becomes evident.

1. *Voice*: The vocal expressions are of dialogical character and are used
   a) for a "gap-song" (a song where gaps are made to be filled in by the child)
   b) to imitate motifs
   c) for mutual exchange of motifs in the sense of a question and answer game.
2. *Relationship*: An interpersonal relationship is ascertainable through mutually referenced vocalisations.
3. *Types of vocal pre-speech expression*: Sound, pitch, rhythm and dynamics of vocal expressions are mutually complemented ("gap-song"), imitated, or reciprocally initiated. A form arises through mutual perception and an increased awareness of vocal expressions.

Modus 6 Joint Experience/Interaffectivity

> The main characteristic is the mutual, playful use of the voice.

1. *Voice*: Child and therapist express themselves vocally in a joint pleasurable game. Often the vocal expressions become associatively connected to imaginary content.
2. *Relationship*: The relationship is playful.
3. *Types of vocal pre-speech expression*: The nonsense syllables, nonsense rhymes and nonsense songs that arise are typical of the playful use of the voice and as a transition to verbal expressions. The mutual emotional and personal expression becomes evident. The dynamics of the vocal expressions are determined by playful affects and/or imaginary content.

tab. 3: Overview of the VQR characteristics

VQR	0	1	2	3	4	5	6
Voice	not perceivable/ rejected	perceived for a short time	functionalized affect dependent	recognized as personal means of expression and explored	is socially referenced	as dialogue	joint playful vocal expressions associations can develop
Relationship	not recognizable	temporary	functionalized	discovery of authorship	inter-intentionality, inter-attentionality are developed social referencing	relationship as dialogue	playful relationship
Vocal pre-speech means of expression	do not appear	vitality affects become vocally audible	vowel-type sounds all parameters are connected to one affect and/or connect the affect no form	exploratory sounds sound, pitch, rhythm, dynamic expression are explored / form develops through the therapist	vowel-consonant connection melodically integrated prefixes proto words connected to gestures form develops through conscious awareness	gap song, mutual taking up of motifs joint form finding	playful use of the voice mutually playful and personal expression free dynamic

IQR: Instrumental Quality of Relationship

> Focus of observation

1. *Instrument*: The duration and way of handling, or the way of playing are assessed with regard to the quality of relationship.
2. *Relationship to object*: Developmental psychological research into the way objects are handled and later how they are played with and related to interpersonal relationships are taken into consideration.
3. *Musical resources*: The way of playing instruments, the approach and expression, are described through analysis of the musical parameters: sound, rhythm, melody, harmony, dynamics and form.
4. *Play space*: Here the play space and especially the musical range on one instrument including the scope in joint playing is assessed.

Modus 0 Lack of Contact/Contact Refusal

> The main characteristic is a lack of reaction to musical instruments. There seems to be either no awareness of the therapist's offer or it is rejected.

1. *Instrument*: The musical instruments in the room are not inviting. Either there seems to be no awareness of the musical instruments or they are rejected. Therapeutical interventions do not lead to any obvious contact-reaction or relationship-stimulating reaction.
2. *Object relationship*: Musical instruments are unable to arouse the child's interest, either as an object or as source of sound.
3. *Musical resources*: The offered instruments do not lead to any obvious positive reaction and are not accepted by the child as a form of expression.
4. *Play space*: No space for playing develops.

Modus 1 Sensory Contact/Contact-Reaction

> The main characteristic is the ability to connect various sensory stimuli, whereby first contact-reaction develops.

1. *Instrument*: Through the incidental handling of an instrument a sound becomes audible. Touching and hearing can lead to a short look at the instrument (contact-reaction). This experience temporarily changes the child's state of affect.

2. *Object relationship*: There is a sensory awareness of the musical instrument. It is used for the child's own sensory needs (touching, smelling, tasting) in a sensory and tactile way. It is not experienced as separated from the child's own body and its function as a means to create sound is not recognized.
3. *Musical resources*: An audible sound can develop by chance through sensory use of the instrument and is briefly perceived by the child.
4. *Play space*: No space for playing develops.

Modus 2 Functionalizing Contact

> The main characteristic is the use of an instrument for one's own affective needs.

1. *Instrument*: The music instrument is functionalized according to the affective state. Either it is:
   a) destructively handled (the music instrument could be damaged) or
   b) played in a stereotyped way.
2. *Object relationship*:
   a) Although the music instrument is recognized as an object, the high affect causes it to be handled destructively, often thrown around or thrown away.
   b) The music instrument is made to make a sound by being played in a stereotyped way.
3. *Musical resources*:
   a) Sound, rhythm and dynamics are determined by a high and unregulated affect. The quality of expression is mainly loud (aggressive-destructive).
   b) The quality of expression is mainly monotonous (stereotype).
      No form develops, which means the beginning and end of playing are not clearly evident.
4. *Play space*: The space for playing is very limited and cannot be further developed.

Modus 3 Contact to Oneself/Self Awareness

> The main characteristic is the intentional explorative handling of a musical instrument that is now recognized in its function as a resonating and sound-making object.

1. *Instrument*: The musical instrument is recognized in its function as a resonating and sound-making object and is explored. The state of affect (tension) which is transferred to the instrument is appropriate to it and to the properties of the material. The instrument can, because of its special quality of sound, cause observable emotional changes in the player.
2. *Object relationship*: The object is recognized as a "musical" instrument. It is made to make a sound in an exploratory way. The child's eyes follow his own actions; the coordination between hand and eyes is evident. The child is aware of himself as author of the sound (authorship).
3. *Musical resources*: Although rhythm, dynamics and expression are influenced by the player's own mood, they are not restricted by it. Rhythmical and melodic motifs become audible. A form can develop by chance or can be brought about with intervention by the therapist, but is not in the foreground.
4. *Play space*: Through exploration of the instrument, scope for playing is opened.

Modus 4 Contact to Another/Intersubjectivity

> The main characteristic is the child's awareness of the therapist while playing.
> The child shows the desire to find confirmation of the experience of his own playing in the therapist (social referencing).

1. *Instrument*: The instrument is played with awareness of its function as the cause of sounds and is related to the playing of the other person and leads to joint attention (inter-attentionality). The social referencing leads to inter-intentionality.
2. *Object relationship*: Joint playing of instrument leads to joint attention (inter-attentionality). Social referencing shows that the experience of togetherness is shared with the therapist.
3. *Musical resources*: Depending on the type of instruments, reciprocal processes of coordination or attunement using timbre, rhythm and pitches can be observed. The playing of the child, who is aware of the therapist's positive confirmation, becomes activated and gains in expression. The beginning and end of joint playing are consciously perceived.
4. *Play space*: The space for play is expanded through the awareness and "letting in" of another in the child's own playing.

Modus 5 Relationship to Another/Interactivity

> The main characteristic is the developed ability to imitate. In playing in the form
> of a dialogue, mutual exchange of motifs, relating to each other as well as making
> pauses, become evident.

1. *Instrument*: The instrument is played dialogically, often in connection with vocal expressions:
   a) imitation of motifs
   b) gap-filling
   c) mutual exchange of motifs, as in question and answer games.
2. *Object relationship*: The musical instrument is consciously played and leads to
   dialogue of longer duration.
3. *Musical resources*:
   a) Rhythmical and melodic motifs are imitated.
   b) The playing takes place in a pre-set musical form.
   c) There is dialogical exchange between the child's playing and the playing of
      another. Rhythmical and melodic motifs are initiated and imitated alternate-
      ly. There is an awareness of dynamics and expression in both players. A form
      develops through increasingly conscious playing and leads to repetition.
4. *Play space*: The play space is shared with another; it is mutually "negotiated".

Modus 6 Joint Experience/Interaffectivity

> The main characteristic is the joint expressive playing that is accompanied by a po-
> sitive emotional state in both players.

1. *Instrument*: The instrument is made to sound in a playful and expressive way,
   whereby the way of playing reflects the characteristics of the instrument and the
   child's state of affect. In this way associations can arise.
2. *Object relationship*: The musical instrument becomes a "playing" instrument.
   The playing reflects a positive emotional state in both players (interaffectivity)
   and can be accompanied by imaginary content.
3. *Musical resources*: The dynamics are free and flexible. A musical form develops
   through the emotional affinity between both players as well as through the arising imaginary content.
4. *Play space*: A joint space for playing develops that is shaped by flowing mutual exchange.

tab. 4: Overview of the IQR characteristics

IQR	0	1	2	3	4	5	6
Instrument	no awareness/ rejected; is not inviting	temporary awareness; function not recognized	functionalised a) destructive b) stereotyped	explored as musical instrument	experience of sound and noise are socially referenced	played in dialogue	expressively played; associations can arise
Object relationship	not noticeable	sensory object relationship	a) affect dependent b) stereotyped	intentional, exploratory playing	inter-intentional/ inter-attentional	instrument serves dialogue	instrument serves joint playing/ expression of imaginary content
Musical resources	no sound	short occurrence of sound, no form	sound, rhythm and dynamics are "restricted"; no melody; no or steretyped form	melodic/rhythmical motifs; focus not on form finding	sound and tonal attunement; rhythmical synchronisation; form develops through awareness of beginning, pauses and end	mutual taking up of motifs; joint form finding	emotional expression; "free" dynamics; form develops through emotional contact and/or through imaginary content
Play space	none	none	limited	is opened	extended	mutually negotiated	joint

TQR: Therapeutic Quality of Relationship

> Focus of observation

1. *Starting point*: the momentary "so-state" of the child, i.e. the situation before the therapist intervenes.
2. *The therapist's state of affect*: The "so-state" of the child causes a specific state of affect to arise in the therapist.
3. *Working hypothesis*: The therapist builds a working hypothesis on the basis of her previous experience of interaction (see "inner working model"), his knowledge of the disorder or disability, music therapeutic intervention techniques and with the help of her intuition.
4. *Focus of intervention*: The intervention of the therapist is based on her working hypothesis and is focussed on a specific aspect of the child's behaviour (mood, movement, state of affect, instrumental/vocal expression).
5. *Intervention*: The "so-state" of the child is intentionally influenced through music therapeutic techniques.
6. *Musical resources*: Here it can be seen which of the musical resources (sound, rhythm, dynamics, melody, harmony, form and expression) is in the foreground.
7. *Play space*: The space for playing is denoted as the space between child and therapist, and is visualized using graphic symbols in the table of characteristics.

Modus 0 The Musical Space/Enveloping

> The main characteristic is a musical form of expression that accepts and surrounds the child in its "so-state". Music is offered with the intention of creating an atmosphere that makes a relationship potentially possible without forcing direct contact. The therapist feels that she is not noticed by child.

1. *Starting point* is the non-reacting child who either shows no contact, rejects the offer of contact, or needs a pause.
2. *The therapist's state of affect*: Because the child does not make any facial or body gestures or other signs that could be seen as acknowledgement of the therapist and acceptance of her offers, she feels she is not noticed.
3. *Working hypothesis*: The therapist presumes that, at this moment in time, the child is unable to show any reaction, but is, however, aware of the atmosphere that the therapist has created in the room.
4. *Focus of intervention*: The therapist is aware of the child's mood but concentrates on the music with which she influences and creates the atmosphere in the room.

5. *Intervention*: Through her musical and facial expression and posture, the therapist makes it possible for her accepting, enfolding stance to be experienced sensorially by the child. The therapist behaves in a way that puts no stress on the child atmospherically. The aim is to surround the "so-state" of the child musically.

6. *Musical resources*: The chosen instruments and the form of playing as well as the voice have no directly inviting character, but rather one of creating resonance. The instruments are mainly long-sounding and are deeply resonant. Rhythms should not be activating. The melodies contain no stimulating motifs. There are no pauses which could contain tension.

7. *Play Space*: The musical playing "envelops" the child. The therapist is aware of the child's physicality, mood and action, but without focussing directly on them.

Modus 1 Connecting Perceptions

> The main characteristic of the therapeutic intervention is the intermodal connection, with which the sensory impressions of the child - feeling, seeing, hearing as well as his body awareness - are brought into attunement.

1. *Starting points* are sensory self-stimulating actions and/or stereotyped movements.

2. *The therapist's state of affect*: The therapist feels challenged to precisely understand the child's movement as well as his physical attributes (body weight and body tension).

3. *Working hypothesis*: Through the coordination of the senses, a contact-reaction develops. The therapist knows that eye contact with the child possibly has no interpersonal meaning. Through an intervention that enables the child to become positively aware of his own body, he becomes calm. Stereotyped movements do not appear at this time.

4. *Focus of intervention*: The therapist focusses her attention directly on the sensory self-stimulating actions and/or the stereotyped movements and the physical state of the child.

5. *Intervention*: The therapist concentrates on the sensory needs and/or stereotyped movements of the child. The musical improvisation develops directly from the child. The rhythm of the child's movement, as well as its intensity, are precisely taken up and made audible. A musical form is developed by the therapist. If the child shows little movement, the rhythm of breathing and body weight of the child are the starting points. If the child permits himself to be touched, carrying, rocking and swinging in the sense of intermodal connection are appropri-

ate. The aim is to help the areas of perception to connect and to enable the child to have synchronised experiences.

6. *Musical resources*: The way of playing is related directly to the movements and the physical state of the child. The rhythm and the contour of intensity must directly reflect both of these to enable synchronised experiences. The therapist finds a musical form that shapes this intervention.

7. *Play space*: The focus is on the child's physicality, so the play space is developed by the therapist starting from the child.

Modus 2 Affect - Affect attunement/Allowing Oneself to be Functionalized

> The main characteristics of the therapeutic intervention are the affect attunement and the shaping of the child's high state of affect by physical, musical and also verbal means. The therapist thereby dedicates herself as a person totally to the child's problems, and in this way feels "functionalized".

1. *Starting point* is a state of high affect and mostly an expression or activity with destructive tendencies on the part of the child.

2. *The therapist's state of affect*: The child's high state of tension causes an equally tense state of affect in the therapist. In some circumstances, she feels threatened or has to protect the instruments. She has to react instantly. Her actions are often observed by the child, who expects sanctions related to his aggressive, destructive actions. The therapist feels that she is being controlled through this behaviour (mainly the corresponding eye contact) and in this way "functionalized".

3. *Working hypothesis*: If the child shows a high state of affect, the therapist must dedicate herself totally to this.

4. *Focus of intervention*: The intervention is completely foccused on the child's state of affect.

5. *Intervention*: If the therapist recognizes the early signals of stress that lead to aggressive behaviour, she regulates these with affect attunement and affect shaping. She communicates to the child that she not only can stand up to the high state of affect, but also can channel it through appropriate playing ideas. The aim of the intervention is for the child to experience the missing affect regulation through another.

6. *Musical resources*: Appropriate to the high state of affect, hard-wearing musical instruments that cannot be damaged are offered. But the instruments must also enable a wide dynamic spectrum to develop (as, for example, the voice), to appropriately express, attune and regulate the state of affect. The musical improvisation (voice, instrumental expression and also the lyrics of improvised songs)

are dynamically and rhythmically tuned exactly to the affective expressions of the child (affect attunement) and formally shaped (affect forming).

7. *Play space*: The atmosphere of the play space is one of high tension. Child and therapist are involved with one another and completely dependent on each other.

Modus 3 Sense of Oneself/Becoming Aware

> The main characteristic of the therapeutic intervention is the intention of making the child aware of his expressions/utterances. The therapist imitates, accompanies, plays around with and sings to these expressions and/or actions of the child to help him become aware of his own body, his voice, his instrumental expression and that he is author of his activities. The therapist feels she is supporting the exploration.

1. *Starting point* is an utterance or action of the child.
2. *The therapist's state of affect*: The therapist is interested in the utterances and actions of the child. This is linked to an appropriately attentive state of affect.
3. *Working hypothesis*: The therapist concentrates on the expressions and/or action of the child and supports them.
4. *Focus of intervention*: The therapist concentrates on the utterances of the child.
5. *Intervention*: The first intervention is primarily listening, through which accompanying, playing with or even reinforcing and exaggerating supports the exploration. Should the child become aware of his body, musically accompanied physical contact could be helpful. If the child discovers his voice, a new sound or invents a motif, the therapist supports this exploration through appropriate instrumental and/or vocal accompaniment. Actions are described and sung about in situation songs. The aim is to strengthen the experience of authorship and self-efficacy and help the child to become aware of important themes.
6. *Musical resources*: The therapist reacts with the same form of expression ("modal") which the child has chosen. Physical expressions become integrated and the child becomes aware of them through sound gestures, body songs and body games. Situation songs are created and describe the momentary activity of the child. Vocal and instrumental expressions are met with a similar timbre. The parameters rhythm, dynamics, melody, harmony and expression are also taken up. By embedding the child's expressions, the therapist develops a repeatable musical form.
7. *Play space*: The play space is filled with the child's expressions and the therapist's supportive interventions.

Modus 4 Intersubjectivity - Being Included as a Person

> The therapist has the experience of being included as a person by the child and can introduce her own ideas for the first time. The main characteristic of the therapeutic intervention is for the therapist to meet the child's need for "social referencing" of his perception and feelings.

1. *Starting point* is the child's initiative to involve the therapist in his playing. It is possible to observe a mutually intended theme from both players and the social-referencing glance.
2. *The therapist's state of affect*: Being involved as a person produces a positive state of affect in the therapist. The first involvement in playing her own ideas is accompanied by a feeling of "release".
3. *Working hypothesis*: The therapist concentrates on something mutual (inter-attentionality). She can bring in her own ideas without breaking the contact. The therapist respects possible pauses made by the child, knowing that he will come into contact again.
4. *Focus of intervention*: The therapist continues to focus her attention on the child's expressions and actions. The child directs his attention towards the therapist and her playing, which can enable a joint theme to develop (inter-attentionality).
5. *Intervention*: The therapist is involved actively in events as an affirmative person. Her interventions now go beyond making the child aware of her expressions and contain for the first time her own ideas. The therapist respects the pauses needed by the child. The aim is to meet the child in his need for social referencing. The musical ideas of the therapist should stimulate the child without aiming at dialogue.
6. *Musical resources*: Improvisation and ways of playing develop from the joint impulse (inter-intentionality) and remain interesting (inter-attentionality) for both players for a long time. The timbre of the chosen instruments can now be more clearly differentiated. The therapist is able to appear as a separate playing partner by means of her own motifs. Musical pauses are also possible.
7. *Play space*: The space for playing becomes clearly more open for the therapist's own playing and is filled with a joint theme.

Modus 5 Musical Dialogue/Musically Answering and Asking

> The main characteristic is the musical dialogue. The therapist considers herself as a person separate from the child and as dialogue partner.

1. *Starting point* is the child's ability to take up and to repeat the therapist's motifs and the child's evident desire for exchange.
2. *The therapist's state of affect*: The therapist is positively involved, which can be seen in her facial expressions and gestures.
3. *Working hypothesis*: The therapist presents herself continually as an individual person with her own desires, ideas and feelings. She expects the child to take up her musical or dance ideas.
4. *Focus of intervention*: The intervention is focussed on the interpersonal interaction.
5. *Intervention*: Dialogues develop from musical answers and questions. The therapist takes up the child's motifs and she experiences that these are answered. The aim is to strengthen the developing interactivity.
6. *Musical resources*: A musical dialogue is characterised by the forms of expression and motifs (movements, rhythms, melodies) that are taken up reciprocally. Imitation and gap-playing are continued through an additional way of playing. Independent motifs draw on each other and give the feeling of talking to each other musically.
7. *Play space*: The space for play is shared by both players: child and therapist.

Modus 6 Play Space - Playing/Having Fun/Imagination

> The main characteristic of the therapeutic intervention is to experience pleasure and fun together with the child. The therapist feels she is a real playing partner

1. *Starting point* is the child's readiness to enter playfully into a relationship.
2. *The therapist's state of affect*: The arising state of pleasure and the fun from playing together lead to a happy, often humorous state of affect.
3. *Working hypothesis*: The therapist is a playing partner and can allow her playful, i.e. musical-dramatic activity, to become more imaginative.
4. *Focus of intervention*: The intervention is focussed on the arising imagination and playing ideas, but above all on the pleasure and fun in playing. The playing is circular.
5. *Intervention*: Playing, role-playing, arising pictures are incorporated into a musically dramatic way of playing. The aim is to approach a theme from the child, or spontaneously arising pictures from the therapist in a playful way.
6. *Musical resources*: Playing with all musical parameters, dancing together, musically dramatic role-playing are characterized by the personal expression and flexible dynamics determined by both players. Pictures and/or important themes of the child arise frequently but are now treated in a playful way.
7. *Play space*: The play space has become a real play space and is filled by both players.

tab. 5: Overview of the TQR characteristics

TQR	0	1	2	3	4	5	6
Starting point	no reaction	sensory stimulating/ stereotyped activity	high affect	exploration	interest in therapist/social referencing	mutual exchange	playful activity
Therapist's state of affect in relation to the child	feels ignored	concentrated	tense	curious/ attentive	relieved	positively involved	pleased, engaged/with humour
Working hypothesis	neutral	as supporter of sensory connections	allows herself to be functionalized	making aware	allows herself to become involved	as dialogue partner	as playing partner
Direction of intervention	music	movement/ body	affect	exploration	common ground	dialogue	play
Musical resources	sound	rhythm	dynamic	child's form of expression	own motifs/ pause	taking up each other's motifs	expression/free dynamics
Intervention	surrounding	sensory connections intermodal	affect attunement/ affect regulation	imitate/ accompany/ playing around the music	own ideas without expectation of a dialogue	answer and question	playing together/ connecting affect and activity/ exchange of roles
Play space							

4. Application of the AQR Tool

4.1. Assessment

What is a "relevant" scene?

It is the therapist's task to identify relevant scenes of a therapy. The question of the relevance of a scene depends on the question and the motive that lead a music therapist to analyse a specific scene from her work with the AQR Tool. Very often an especially successful therapy situation is seen as relevant, because it illustrates an evident change in the quality of relationship. Just as relevant, however, are sequences that show typical continually recurring types of behaviour that do not lead to the expected therapeutic success. In this way, a scene in which the therapist feels completely helpless can be analysed as relevant. It is crucial to be able to formulate in a comprehensive way the reasons for the choice of a scene and to connect the results of the analysis to the original question. Experience shows that sequences of 1 to 3 minutes are enough to comprehend an existing quality of relationship. Only then is the question asked concerning how often this modus arises in a therapy session or in the course of therapy.

Which scale is applied?

Which of the four scales should be applied for the analysis is decided by the kind of questions and the means of expression that are in the foreground. When there is no instrumental or vocal expression, the child's physical-emotional expression is in the foreground. Where vocal or instrumental expression arises, the vocal pre-speech or instrumental scale is applied. One of the most important questions in the assessment of the quality of relationship is whether the therapist uses the appropriate intervention (method) for the momentary state of the child. An assessment according to the TQR Scale helps to determine the therapist's working model that can be seen in her interventions. If one puts the assessed modus of the TQR Scale in relation to an assessment of the physical-emotional and/or the child's vocal or instrumental expression, it becomes evident whether the therapist has determined the child's state of development and has applied the appropriate intervention. Possible intervention mistakes can, in this way, be recognized and the method changed. Frequent intervention mistakes are described in the section "Guidelines for the assessment".

How is an assessment made?

Each scale is preceded by a description of the main points of focus. It has proved useful, in the first place, to make one's own observations on these focal points. Here, it can quickly be seen which modi are not relevant. The summarized text that precedes each modus as the main characteristic is helpful for deciding on the "correct" modus. After the scene has been watched repeatedly, one's perception can be reviewed according to the list of characteristics and an assessment can be reached. The tables at the end of each scale summarize the characteristics and enable trained users of the AQR Tool to have a quick overview.

Time required

The more the therapist is trained and experienced in the application of the AQR Tool, the more sure and economical she becomes in making and describing the assessment during the therapy sessions as well as in their documentation.

What are basic qualities and peaks?

A modus that often arises and is clearly established is described as the "basic modus". With new or only shortly arising qualities, we talk of so-called "peaks". Peaks do not only indicate potential possibilities but also the patient's limits. There must be awareness of these, especially if they are short and irregular. It is important to react to stress signs with the appropriate intervention.

4.2. The AQR Tool in the course of therapy

At the beginning of therapy, while forming the diagnosis, the AQR Tool can be applied in order to determine the ability for relationships. Furthermore, it can be used for the analysis of single sequences or the representation of a course of therapy (evaluation, documentation). The analysis of selected sequences with the AQR Tool can also help in the development of appropriate aims of therapy (prognosis). In this way, a comparison of the course of therapy is possible (research) when studying various cases with the same diagnosis. Within the therapy situation itself, a quick assessment of the patient's ability for relationship leads to an appropriate and good intervention. The "hour glass" shows a possible approach to the application of the AQR Tool in overview.

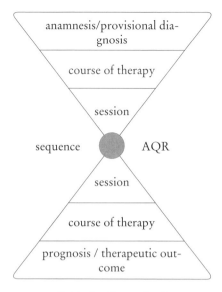

fig 5.: the "hour glass"

First contact/diagnosis

After considering the medical indication made by a doctor or a psychologist, an an-amnesis is also made by a music therapist through meetings with the parents. In the first (probatory) sittings, the AQR Tool can be applied to verify the indication and to increase the observations that possibly were unable to be made through other test and diagnostic methods. In addition, relevant scenes are selected that depend on the kinds of questions asked. Diagnostic questions that can be answered with the help of an assessment are, for example:

- What is the quality of the child's ability for interpersonal relationships?
- What is the child's emotional-cognitive age of development?
- How can his physical-emotional expression be assessed?
- How can his vocal pre-speech expression be assessed?
- Is the object-relationship to instruments already developed?
- Which emotional quality accompanies the playing of musical instruments?

The application of the AQR Tool in the field of diagnosis has already been seen in other work. Therefore, its use in complementing other diagnostic procedures, for example, OPD II in work with adults (Körber, 2009) and in work with children (Burghardt-Distl, 2009) has already been described.

Course of therapy

In the course of therapy, the therapist is motivated to select "relevant scenes" through a specific line of questioning. Frequent questions are: from which point in time did a type of behaviour change or when did a new theme arise and what caused this? One way is to run quickly through the usually extensive video material to hit upon sequences that show "the new". Another way to have an overview of the course of therapy is to use graphic representation in which basic modi and peaks of a session are illustrated (see chapter "Visualisation"). Here it can also be of interest to examine the process that led to a change.

Sequence

If a specific modus is confirmed in a sequence, it is important to look for this modus quantitatively in the course of therapy. In this way, it can be confirmed if it relates to a basic quality in the sense of a clearly developed modus or to a peak, i.e. a quality that arises for a short time and stands out from the usual behaviour. Experience shows that the therapist has a feeling for this assessment after each session. However, verification through video analysis can also uncover "intuitive" moments that are no longer in the therapist's memory.

Prognosis/result of therapy

Looking over the documentation which has been made with the help of the AQR Tool, one can quickly get an overview of when and in which context specific modi are named. It soon becomes evident if a very long period on one level of development is observed, and if quick changes in the qualities or a constant increase in the ability for relationship can be observed. These assessments can be considered together with the primary diagnosis and the presumed continuation of the course of development.

Therapy plans always contain questions of therapy success and prognosis. In order to answer these for music therapy, it is necessary to translate the descriptions of the AQR modi into a language that the reader (doctor, therapist, social worker etc.) understands whereby knowledge of developmental psychology forms a common basis.

4.3. Guidelines for the assessment

An important aim of assessment with the AQR Tool is the improvement of the therapeutic intervention technique. The aim of this section is to point out common errors in interventions and mistaken interpretations of the child's behaviour. The remarks on individual modi end with the formulation of a working model, which should make clear the therapist's positive attitude towards each stage of development.

Advice on Modus 0

The reason for the child's non-reaction could be the need for a pause that is necessary for the processing of what he has experienced, and to stabilize affects (see also advice on modi 1 and 4). If the child reacts with rejection by, for example, pushing an instrument away (modus 0), this must be distinguished from a way of handling the instrument charged with affect (modus 2) that could lead to damage of the instrument.

Feelings of isolation, fear or inner emptiness could develop in the therapist if she feels the child has no awareness of her. This could prevent an attitude of acceptance and the appropriate intervention for the state of development of the child. For the therapist's state of affect, her experience and her assessment of the psychopathology play an important role. They help to overcome disappointment over the failure to make progress in developing contact or over contact breaking off.

The therapist should show a calm state of affect in her facial expression, posture and in her musical expression. She can emphasize different aspects of playing. She can either play:
- for the atmosphere in the room (forming a "musical room")
- for the child (without focussing on his mood or movement)
- or for herself to relieve the pressure of the relationship level. Especially when the child makes a pause, playing for herself is a good solution for the therapist, in order not to build up an attitude of expectation.

> The Therapist's Working Model:
> The therapist is not resentful that the child cannot be aware of her.

Advice on Modus 1

The child has to have enough sensory experiences with the help of his "near senses" (such as touch/feel, smell, taste) because the sensory abilities from near senses are necessary for the "far senses" (such as hearing and sight) to develop. For example, the sensory perception of an instrument (modus 1) is to be differentiated from the exploration of an instrument (modus 3). Hand-eye coordination is a clear characteristic of exploration of an instrument.

With reference to the reactions of the child, there must be a differentiation between obvious reactions, discrete reactions in the sense of weak, fleeting reactions, and actions that presumably would have happened without the therapist's intervention. In addition, in the assessment of the "short term", the individual feeling for the child's sense of time must be considered. If there is a glance, it is important to evaluate the quality and direction of this glance carefully. The glance can either
- be directed towards the "source of sound" (this can also in some cases be the therapist if she has expressed herself vocally) as though to ask: "Where did the sound come from?" (modus 1) or

- be directed towards the therapist as though to ask: "Did you also experience what I experienced?" (modus 4).

If the therapist wants to experience the child's reaction again or misinterprets a child's glance as intersubjective exchange, the result can be overstimulation of the child. This can be seen in interventions that take too much time, or in a basic attitude that does not relate to the momentary relationship modus of the child. If the child cannot withstand this, a breaking off of contact can be the result. If the therapist recognizes the glance of the child as the result of a successful connection of the senses, she leads his intervention to an end and enables the child to have a pause to process what he has experienced.

Research by Jones et al. (2008) shows that two-year old children on the autistic spectrum, in comparison to normally developed children and to children with delayed development, direct their attention towards the eyes of others much less often. In fact, in comparison to the control group, the attention was directed more frequently to the mouth of a speaking person. As a possible explanation, Jones cites the synchronicity of the visual and audible stimulation.

The interventions "intermodal connection" (modus 1) and "affect attunement" (modus 2) must be clearly differentiated. For intermodal connection, the therapist focusses on the rhythm and form of the child's movement. However, if she takes the intensity of the movement as the starting point, the focus is on the affect (modus 2).

The Therapist's Working Model:
The therapist dedicates herself totally to the sensory needs of the child.

Advice on modus 2

The functionalizing of the therapist ranges from the child displaying a high and "dangerous" affect, which causes the therapist to react immediately, to dictating specific activities that the therapist should do. The child has to use the therapist for his needs until he has internalised the experience of being author of a situation. If the therapist is angry about "being functionalized", this can prevent her from dedicating herself completely to the child's needs. Only when the child has had enough experience of his self-efficacy does his need become milder and appear less frequently in the course of therapy.

If the child shows high affects, the evaluation of this in relation to the appropriate intervention is decisive. High affects do not always have to be "dangerous". However, if the therapist is physically threatened by the child, or if instruments could be damaged, she must primarily protect herself and the instruments through physical distance. For the further course of therapy, it is important to confront the child's urgent emotional needs with affect attunement and affect forming. Affect attunement is one of the most difficult interventions, as the therapist could possibly lose the control over her own state of affect. This leads to intervention mistakes if the therapist does not recognize and attune exactly to the too high affect, and instead either exaggerates, calms it too quickly, appeases or does not take the affect seriously. If the therapist cannot really recognize the child's affect, the intervention of affect attunement is not effective, or even contra-productive. In addition, an affect attunement without form can raise the aggressive affect instead of recognising it and thereby calming it. However, if the high affect can be shared and regulated through the interventions of the therapist, the child's functionalising behaviour becomes less and less in the further course of therapy.

Other intervention techniques such as providing security through physical holding, a calm voice without demands or interpretation of behaviour as well as unchallenging surroundings can be helpful depending on the degree of high affect. If high affects are caused by lack of appropriate expression and ability for communication, providing means of expression that stand up to this high affect are crucial.

> The Therapist's Working Model:
> The therapist is able to put herself completely at the child's disposal.

Advice on modus 3

For the development of the child's voice, it is important to evaluate whether he is aware of his expressions as something "own, self-made". Only then is it useful to imitate or accompany etc. the child's vocal expressions. If the child is exploring a long sounding instrument, his listening can lead to a break in play. This is characterised by concentration on the sound experience. It is important that the therapist is aware of the child's ability for exploration, gives this enough room and does not engage the child in dialogue too soon. Therefore, it is not helpful to seek or force eye contact.

> The Therapist's Working Model:
> The therapist can dedicate herself completely to the child's exploration.

Advice on modus 4

The feeling of being recognized as a person can mislead the therapist into wanting to react too quickly as a dialogue partner. Another intervention mistake can develop if the therapist experiences the child's pauses as break of contact and tries to force new contact too hastily.

> The Therapist's Working Model:
> The therapist feels there is awareness of her as a person.

Advice on modus 5

The filling of a "gap" can only be assessed here with modus 5 if this ability repeatedly arises. If the child imitates the therapist's expressions, there is a need to differentiate between this and echolalia.

The shared feeling of time is decisive for dialogical play(ing). This is recognisable through the respective duration of play and the exchange of pauses. If the therapist is afraid that the dialogue play(ing) is lost again, she frequently reacts too quickly to the child's impulses and therefore does not find appropriate timing. This is also frequently an indication that the child's ability for dialogue is not yet properly developed.

One can also observe whether the child's emotional reactions are appropriate to the therapist's interventions or whether the child tries to regulate himself or shows signs of stress.

> The Therapist's Working Model:
> The therapist reacts and acts as dialogue partner.

Advice on modus 6

Initially, the child's actions can cause associations in the therapist. She can then integrate these actions into pictures, stories etc. For the therapist, it is important to be aware from what point in time these kinds of pictures arise in herself.

In playing, affect and activity are connected. Because the inability to experience the connection between affect and activity is a typical characteristic of autistic spectrum disorder, it is one of the most important experiences to develop games in which activity and affect build a unity. Therefore, it is important to pay attention to whether the child's theme must be played (modus 2) or if the child can develop in a "free" way of playing. In free playing the child plays the affect (modus 6) and the affect does not control the child (modus 2).

Nevertheless, it is important, especially here, to be mindful of the affect regulation in order to continue to stabilise the developing relationship. Positive high affects have above all to be shared. The therapist pays attention to maintaining the integration of this positive atmosphere for the child and finds a form of playing that enables the shaping of these affects. The experience of interactivity requires long-term support.

> The Therapist's Working Model:
> The therapist is a playing partner.

5. Visualisation

With the development of the AQR Tool there were ideas for the graphic representation of individual aspects right from the beginning: The musician Manfred Hüneke transcribed musical sequences from music therapy and presented them in conventional notation as well as graphically (Hüneke in: Schumacher, 1999). For the DVD "Synchronisation - In Search of Shared Time" (Hüneke in: Schumacher & Calvet, 2008) he created graphic notation which demonstrated synchronous moments in the improvised music.

In Silke Reimer's article "Kurzzeitige Wechsel von Beziehungsqualitäten" [Short-term Changes in the Quality of Relationship] (Reimer, 2004) a sequence of two and a half minutes is analysed and a microanalysis of the instrumental expression is shown graphically. In a lecture about the application of the AQR Tool in work with severely multiply disabled adults (Reimer, 2010), this approach was taken up again and further developed in collaboration with the communication and social scientist Lada Petrickova for this publication. In the basic model of the graphic representation there are seven rows which represent the modi 0–6 as well as circles which represent the scales with various colours and letters. Peaks are indicated by arrows.

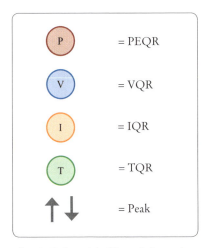

fig. 6: Colour labelling of the scales

As described in the chapter on the application of the AQR Tool, the main question in an assessment is mostly whether the therapist's intervention is adequately adapted to the developmental state of the child. The graphic representation of such an assessment can highlight this aspect. The following graphic example shows the assessment of a scene in which the child's behaviour and the therapist's intervention diverge at first, but shortly afterwards come together.

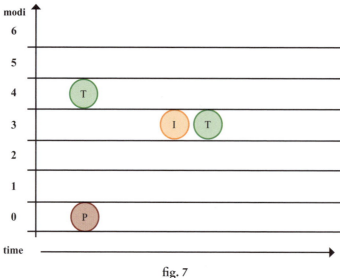

fig. 7

The therapist offers the child a movement game to play together (TQR modus 4), with which the child, however, cannot involve himself in any way (PEQR modus 0). Shortly afterwards, the child plays on the piano (IQR modus 3) and the therapist accompanies this activity (TQR modus 3).

For the graphic representation of the child's state of development within a chosen sequence, of one session (also diagnosis) or of a course of therapy, all three scales (PEQR, VQR and IQR) can be included in the visualisation next to each other. The following visualisation shows an assessment of the child's basic qualities of relationship regarding his physical-emotional, his vocal and his instrumental expression.

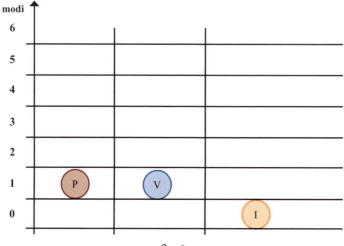

fig. 8

Even though only the state of development of the child is graphically presented here, it should be taken into consideration that the behaviour of the child is always to be seen within the close context of the therapeutic interventions. As well as the possibilities shown with this graphic model, whole sessions can be represented graphically. The qualities of relationship that predominantly arise during a session are notated as basic modi and developmental tendencies or peaks are shown with arrows. Modi that are just beginning to develop can be illustrated with smaller circles. When graphic representation is continued in this way, it can quickly demonstrate when, for example, a specific behaviour arises for the first time or if the basic modus changes over a longer period of time in the course of therapy.

With microanalysis, an assessment of behaviour and its duration timed exactly to the second is needed. Here, instead of circles, blocks of colour are used that demonstrate the exact duration of a modus. The following visualisation shows the child and the therapist illustrated as in a musical score in two staves. In the graphic representation, the x-axis is the timeline. The following example shows minute 1.20 to 2.42 of a sequence.

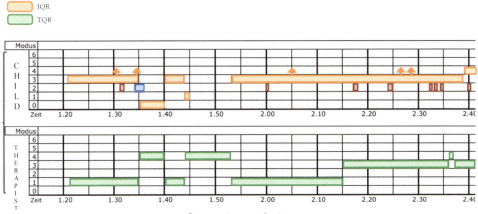

fig. 9: microanalysis

Here the child's intentional instrumental playing is predominant (IQR modus 3) and is briefly interrupted at minute 1.35 (IQR modus 0). At minute 1.44, a further instrument makes a sound through accidental touching (IQR modus 1). Then the child returns to the intentional playing (IQR modus 3). At minutes 1.31, 1.34, 2.15, 2.27 and 2.29, the child glances towards the therapist (peaks in modus 4). At minute 2.37, the child seems to play some wrong notes and after this creates a proper ending and looks at the therapist (modus 4). During the whole sequence, signs of stress arise (PEQR modus 2). Tension is also heard in a vocal utterance (VQR modus 2).

The therapist bounces on the trampoline in time with the rhythm of the piano playing (TQR modus 1, as in intermodal connection). Every time the child interrupts his playing, the therapist also interrupts her movement in order to enable a joint pause (TQR modus 4). At minute 2.15, she begins to accompany the child's playing vocally and with body percussion (modus 3). At minute 2.36, she temporarily doubles the rhythm (modus 4) but returns immediately to the basic rhythm (modus 3). Towards the end of the sequence she changes the sound of her clapping and in this way clearly supports the way the child finalises his playing.

Through the use of appropriate technology, further possibilities arise e.g. animated pictures for presentations or DVDs. Examples of this can be found in a publication on music therapy for people with dementia (Muthesius et al., 2010).

Software for data evaluation e.g. "Interact" (Mangold, 2010) offers several possibilities for visualisation. For example, basic qualities and peaks can be illustrated with blocks or pie diagrams (see figure below) which illustrate the duration of various behaviours.

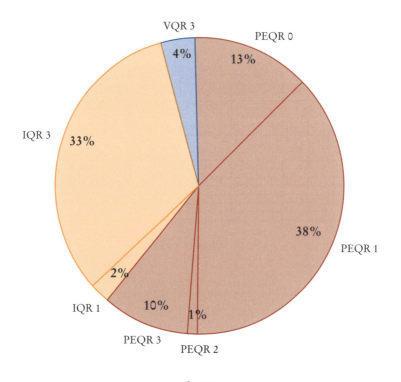

fig. 10

6. Outlook

6.1. Speech scale – previously modus 7

Readers of the earlier publications on the AQR Tool will have realised that modus 7 (Verbalising/Reflecting) does not appear in this revision of the AQR Tool as it needs its own scale. An elaboration could be as follows: if a verbal expression arises, this must also be assessed in its quality of relationship in a differentiated way. The assessment can therefore also follow the logic of developmental psychology based modi. According to Stern's self-concept, the basis for "verbal and the narrative self" is laid.

SQR Scale for the assessment of verbal expression
Modus 0 – no verbal expression
Modus 1 – short, rare verbal expression
Modus 2 – functionalizing speech
Modus 3 – intentional verbal expression
Modus 4 – expression directed to and including the other
Modus 5 – verbal dialogue
Modus 6 – verbal games, association
Modus 7 – reflection

As in the scales presented here which refer to the preverbal time, the theoretical basis for the acquisition of speech and the possible disturbances must be worked out according to the clinical picture. Only on this basis can appropriate characteristics of each modus be formulated.

6.2. Documentation and diagnostics

Results of the certificate courses up to now show that the AQR Tool can be applied above all for checking therapeutic interventions and for clinical supervision. In addition, there is great interest in an application for diagnostic and documentation uses. The Music-Based Scale for Autism Diagnostics (MUSAD; Bergmann et al., 2015b) is an observational tool based on data gained from the application of the AQR Tool. The MUSAD is well suited to assessing individuals with speech impairments on a lower level of developmental functioning and shows promising psychometric properties (Bergmann et al., 2015a).

6.3. Research

In Reimer's book about affect regulation (Reimer, 2016) the AQR Tool was used to assess video examples from music therapy with people with severe multiple disabilities. The results show that developmentally oriented music therapy has positive effects on the emotional state and therefore on the contact and the ability to relate. The book lays the foundation for a theory-based application of music therapeutic interventions when working with people with severe multiple disabilities.

The AQR Tool also was used as an observation and assessment tool within an international research project conducted by the Grieg Academy Music Therapy Research Centre (Bergen, Norway) in collaboration with the Berlin University of the Arts from 2013–2017. This project examined the quality of the therapeutic relationship as a predictor of the development of social-emotional skills in children with autism spectrum disorder. Initial results showed that a therapeutic relationship, in which the therapist attunes to the child's expressions musically and emotionally, seems to be an important mediator of generalized social skills, as observed by independent assessors as well as by parents in natural settings (Mössler et al., 2017).

6.4. Music and dance education

The clear structure, easy applicability, high significance for the music therapy process and the universality of its access led to the idea of using the AQR Tool in the field of music and dance pedagogy, especially in inclusive settings. Since the AQR Tool has been designed and developed for music therapy, changes and/or extensions are necessary for the application in the field of music and dance education.

A research project at the Orff Institute of the Mozarteum University Salzburg (Austria) is therefore working on an adaption of the AQR Tool for pedagogical use. This concerns the assessment of the developmental level and the child's ability to relate as well as the educational interventions. The content and methodical decisions of teachers in (elemental) music and dance teaching should be subject to critical, empirical consideration with regard to their influence and their effect on the quality of the relationship of children in heterogeneous learning groups.

The results of these studies will produce a substantial and novel contribution to qualitative teaching research in the field of artistic-pedagogical and inclusive contexts. They are intended to deliver information about ways to react to various levels of interaction (in the sense of interaction abilities and possibilities) and about which of the applied artistic-educational interventions may prove to be beneficial.

Finally, the adaption of the AQR Tool should be able to provide recommendations in critical situations. Based on this, together with the educators involved, the question of appropriate educational interventions (in the sense of improving the quality of relationship) should be pursued in specific learning situations.

In this way, the AQR Tool could be used as a guide to pedagogical practice to show which interventions generate which effects, how the quality of relationship can be strengthened or changed and which interventions are most suited to the respective development level of the children.

7. Glossary

Affect attunement: a behavior that is more than imitation, mirroring and empathy that happens normally unconsciously, almost automatically. A form of intersubjectivity which takes "the experience of emotional resonance and automatically recasts that experience into another form of expression" (Stern, 1985, p. 144–145). Most attunements occur across sensory modes (ibid., p. 148) with three dimensions – intensity, timing and shape – specific across the matches of behavior (ibid., p. 146). It focuses on the reflecting and sharing of inner states, allows the infant to "recognize that internal states are forms of human experience" (ibid., p. 151). In this publication "affect attunement" means a therapeutic intervention (TQR Modus 2) in which the therapist exactly attunes to the child with his improvisation in absolute intensity, intensity contour, temporal beat, rhythm, duration and shape.

Affect regulation: here an intervention for the regulation of the child's high affect.

Amodal perception: "(…) the capacity to transfer perceptual experience from one sensory modality to another." (Stern, 1985, p. 47). The function is to connect experiences.

Authorship: see self-agency

Ability for relationship: belongs to the innate make-up of a human being and involves the ability to react emotionally to each other.

Attachment: attachment theory was developed by the British child psychiatrist John Bowlby. Attachment describes a life-long need to build close and emotionally intensive relationships to other people. Attachment remains "active throughout the life cycle" (Holmes, 1996, p. 181).

Background feelings: arise from background emotions, and these emotions, also more internally than externally directed, are observable to others in myriad ways: body postures, the speed and design of our movements, and even the tone of our voices and the prosody in our speech as we communicate thoughts that may have little to do with the background emotions (Damasio, 1994/1999).

Core Self: develops through the sense of being a complete physical whole and is known as "self-coherence". It includes "self-agency" in the sense of being author of one's own actions; "self-affectivity" meaning the experience of regular emotional qualities; "self-history" meaning a sense of continuity (Stern, 2000, p. 71). This version of Stern's book "The Interpersonal World of the Infant" (2000) contains a differentiation of core-self.

Contact-Reaction: the result of a successful intermodal connection.

Echolalia: vocal and instrumental expressions that are repeated like an echo until meaningless.

Imitation: the imitation of human behaviour is a prerequisite for the development of empathy. Imitation embraces the appreciable quality of feeling underlying the behaviour, whereas mimicry remains concentrated on the external visible behaviour. Deferred imitation (Piaget, 1952) requires not only the ability for reproduction but also long-term memory.

Inner working models (IWM): internal representation of interaction experiences in order to anticipate events in the real world and to plan behaviour in a foresighted way (Fremmer-Bombik, 1997, p. 109). With the aid of working models, the individual perceives and interprets events, forecasts the future, and constructs plans (Bretherton, 2002, p. 1066) so that a person can plan his behaviour in a foresighted way and avoid having false expectations. Working models reveal something about the quality of attachment (Grossmann, 1997, p. 58) , which is different in every person and develop from the experiences of availability and/or rejection by the caregiver (Spangler/Zimmermann, 1999, p. 172). These models regulate attachment behaviour and feelings. The quality of attachment also affects later relationships and is therefore of long duration. In this publication, the term is used together with the therapist's working hypothesis and describes his previous interaction experience with children with pervasive developmental disturbances.

Intentional activity: a conscious and deliberate action.

Interaffectivity: "(…) a match between the feeling state as experienced within and as seen "'on' or 'in' another (…). Interactivity may be the first, most pervasive, and most immediately important form of sharing subjective experiences." (Stern, 2000, p. 132).

Interactivity: mutual listening, seeing and sensing of another and reacting and/or responding to his activity.

Inter-attentionality: joint focussing of the attention of the child and the caregiver on the same point (Stern, 2000, p. 130).

Inter-intentionality: By the age of nine months, "Intentions have become shareable experiences". Infants attribute a mental state to another, "namely the comprehension of their intentions and the capacity to satisfy that intention" (Stern, 2000, p. 131).

Intermodal Connection: an intervention which brings the sensory perceptions hearing, feeling, seeing in attunement. The aim of intermodal connection is to help connect areas of perception and to enable the child to have synchronous experiences.

Intersubjectivity: psychological intimacy, meaning to entrust subjective experiences to another and to recognize them in the other. "(…) sharing of subjective experience between self and other and the influencing of one another's subjective experience." (Stern, 2000, p. 203)

Intervention technique: targeted influence of the therapist based on his musical and psychotherapeutic tools

Intrasynchronisation: the temporal structures in a person's body are attuned to each other, which means that facial expression, body (limbs, torso) move in a fraction of a second in exact attunement. As soon as vocal expression is added, this is also co-ordinated with the body's movement.

OPD-2: German Psychodynamic Diagnostic system as an addition to the existing psychiatric diagnosis manuals. It adds some fundamental psychodynamic dimensions to the description-oriented classification of mental disorders (Arbeitskreis OPD, 2006. English version see: OPD Task Force 2008).

Pause: a strategy to process the intensity of an experience.

Peak: a momentary appearance of a quality of relationship (in contrast to the so-called basic modus). In mathematics "peak" describes high and/or low points of graphic representations of curves.

Physicality: Within the TQR Scale and the PEQR Scale, the following are important: the weight of the child, his posture and body tension (tone).

Proprioception: In the TQR Scale and PEQR Scale we take this to mean one's own body perception and body awareness.

Self-agency: in the sense of authorship of one's own actions and non-authorship of the actions of the others; having volition, having control over self-generated action (your arm moves when you want it to), and expecting consequences of one's actions (when you shut your eyes it gets dark) (Stern, 2000, p. 71).

Self-affectivity: experiencing patterned inner qualities of feelings (affects) that belong with other experiences of self (Stern, 2000, p. 71).

Self-coherence: having a sense of being a non-fragmented, physical whole with boundaries and a locus of integrated action, both while moving and when still (Stern, 2000, p. 71).

Self-history (memory): the capacity to remember the continuity of experience through memory (Stern, 2000, p. 90).

Sense of an emergent self: "a sense of organization in the process of formation" (Stern, 2000, p. 38), formed during the first two months. "It concerns the learning about the relations between the infant's sensory experiences" (Stern, 2000, p. 46). With the help of innate and acquired abilities, relationships between the sensory experiences are created whereby a first feeling of regularity and order are experienced.

Sensitivity: the ability to recognize the child's signals and to interpret them correctly, and when this has been grasped, to react appropriately and promptly (Ainsworth, 1978, p. 312).

Situation Song: a made-up song that sings about the child's momentary activity and/or his mood.

Social referencing: Infants can "attribute shareable affective states to their social partners" (Stern, 2000, p. 131). Feeling uncertain, infants "look towards mother to read her face for its affective content, essentially to see what they should feel, to get a second appraisal to help resolve their uncertainty" (Stern, 2000, p. 132).

So-state: the physical and emotional state of the patient as he appears at the present moment to the therapist before she starts to intervene (Schumacher, K. et al., 2017).

Vitality affects: a quality of experience that can arise directly from encounters with people (Stern, 2000, p. 54). In contrast to Darwin's categorical affects such as anger, pleasure, sadness etc., it is characterized by dynamic, kinetic terms such as "surging", "fading away", "fleeting", "explosive", "crescendo", "bursting", "drawn out", and so on". (ibid).

8. References

Ainsworth, M. D. S., & Bell, S. M. (1974). Mother-infant interaction and the development of competence. In: K. Connolly & J. S. Brunner (Eds.), *The growth of competence*. London and New York: Academic Press.

Ainsworth, M. D. S., Blehar, M. C., Waters, E., & Wall, S. (1978). *Patterns of Attachment: A Psychological Study of the Strange Situation*. Hillsdale, NJ: Erlbaum.

Als, H., Lester, B. M., Tronick, E. C., & Brazelton, T. B. (1982). Manual for assessment of preterm infant behavior (APIB). In: Fitzgerald, H. E., Lester, B. M., Yogman, M. Y. (Eds.): *Theory and research in behavioural paediatrics, 1, 35–63)*. New York.

Als, H. (1986): A synactive model of neonatal Behavioral Organization. Framework for the Assessment of Neurobehavioral Development in the Premature Infant and for Support of Infants and Parents in the Neonatal Intensive Care Environment. In: Sweeney (ed.): *The high-risk neonate. Developmental therapy perspectives*. New York: Haworth Press.

Arbeitskreis OPD-KJ (Hrsg.) (2003). *Operationalisierte Psychodynamische Diagnostik im Kindes- und Jugendalter*. Grundlagen und Manual. Bern: Huber.

Arbeitskreis OPD (Hrsg.) (2006). *Operationalisierte Psychodynamische Diagnostik OPD-2.* Das Manual für Diagnostik und Therapieplanung. Bern: Huber.

Bergmann, T., Sappok, T., Diefenbacher, A., Dames, S., Heinrich, M., Ziegler, M., & Dziobek, I. (2015a). Music-based Autism Diagnostics (MUSAD): A newly developed diagnostic measure for adults with intellectual developmental disabilities suspected of autism. *Research in Developmental Disabilities*, 43–44, 123–135. doi:10.1016/j.ridd.2015.05.011.

Bergmann, T., Sappok, T., Diefenbacher, A., & Dziobek, I. (2015b). Music in diagnostics: Using musical interactional settings for diagnosing autism in adults with intellectual developmental disabilities. *Nordic Journal of Music Therapy, 25*(4), 319–351. doi:10.1080/08098131.2015.1039567.

Bowlby, J. (1951). *Maternal care and mental health.* World Health Organisation, Monograph Series No. 2.

Bowlby, J. (1969). *Attachment and loss*. Vol. 1: Attachment. New York: Basic Books.

Bowlby, J. (1979). *The making and breaking of affectional bonds*. London: Tavistock Publications.

Bowlby, J. (1998). *A Secure Base*. New York: Basic Books.

Brazelton, T. B. (1973). Neonatal Behavioral Assessment Scale. *Clinics in Developmental Medicine*, 50. Philadelphia: JB Lippincott.

Bretherton, I. (2002). Bindungsbeziehungen und Bindungsrepräsentationen in der frühen Kindheit und im Vorschulalter: Überlegungen zu dem Konstrukt des Inneren Arbeitsmodells. In: K. Brisch, K. Grossmann, K. Grossmann, & L. Koehler (Eds.). Bindungen und seelische Entwicklungswege: Vorbeugung, Interventionen und klinische Praxis, *13–46*. Stuttgart: Klett-Cotta.

Brisch, K. H. (2008). Der Säugling – Bindung, Neurobiologie und Gene. Stuttgart: Klett-Cotta.

Bruner, J. (1979). Learning How to Do Things with Words. In D. Aaranson & R. W. Rieber. *Psycholinguistic Research: Implications and Applications, 265–284.* Hillsdale, NJ: Erlbaum.

Bruner, J. (1982). The beginning of request. In: K. Nelson (Ed.). *Children's language, 91–138.* Hillsdale, NJ: Erlbaum.

Burghardt-Distl, A. (2009). Der diagnostische Nutzen des Instruments zur Einschätzung der Beziehungsqualität (EBQ) für den Kinderbereich. Eine Abhandlung an Hand wissenschaftlicher Kriterien und einer musiktherapeutisch-psychologischen Einzelfallanalyse. *Musiktherapeutische Umschau, 30/2009, 2.*

Butterworth, G. E. (1989). Hand-mouth co-ordination in the new-born human infant. *British Journal of Developmental Psychology, 6 (4), 303–314.*

Butterworth, G. E. (1998). What is special about pointing? In F. Simion & G. E. Butterworth (Eds.): *The development of sensory motor and cognitive capacities in early infancy: From perception to cognition.* Hove: Psychology Press.

Calvet-Kruppa, C. (2001). Feinfühligkeit als Interaktionsqualität. Ein Leitfaden entwicklungspsychologischer Intervention. In: O. Decker & A. Borkenhagen (Hrsg.) *Psychoanalyse, Texte zur Sozialforschung, 9, 153–156.*

Calvet-Kruppa, C., Ziegenhain, U., & Derksen, B. (2005). Kinder mit Down-Syndrom: Entwicklungspsychologische Elternberatung. In Jürgen Kühl (Hrsg.). *Autonomie und Dialog - kleine Kinder in der Frühförderung,* 80–86. München, Reinhardt.

Condon, W. S. (1963). *Synchrony units and the communicational hierarchy.* Paper presented at Western Psychiatric Institute. Pittsburgh, Pa.

Crittenden, P. C. (1996). Entwicklung, Erfahrung und Beziehungsmuster: Psychische Gesundheit aus bindungstheoretischer Sicht. *Praxis der Kinderpsychologie und Kinderpsychiatrie,* 45, 147–155.

Crittenden, P. M. (2000). A dynamic-maturational approach to continuity and change in pattern of attachment. In: P. M. Crittenden and A. H. Claussen (Eds). *The organization of attachment relationships: Maturation, culture, and context,* 343–357. New York: Cambridge University Press.

Damasio, A. R. (1994). *Descartes' error: Emotion, reason and the human brain.* New York: G. P. Putnam's Sons.

Damasio, A. R. (1999). *The feeling of what happens: Body and emotion in the making of consciousness.* New York: Harcourt Brace.

D'Entremont, B, Hains, S. M. J., & Muir, D. W. (1997). A demonstration of gaze following in 3 to 6 months olds. *Infant behavior and development,* 20 (4), 569–572.

Derksen, B., & Lohmann, S. (2009). *Baby-Lesen.* Die Signale des Säuglings lesen und verstehen. Stuttgart: Hippokrates.

Fonagy, P. (1998). Die Bedeutung der Entwicklung metakognitiver Kontrolle der mentalen Repräsentanzen für die Betreuung und das Wachstum des Kindes. *Psyche,* 4, 348–368.

Fonagy P. (2001). *Attachment Theory and Psychoanalysis.* New York: Other Press.

Fremmer-Bombik, E. (1997). Innere Arbeitsmodelle von Bindung. In: Spangler, G., & Zimmermann, P. (Hrsg.). *Die Bindungstheorie.* Stuttgart: Klett-Cotta.

Frohne-Hagemann, I., & Pleß-Adamczyk, H. (2004). *Indikation Musiktherapie bei psychischen Problemen im Kindes- und Jugendalter.* Musiktherapeutische Diagnostik und Manual nach ICD-10. Göttingen: Vandenhoeck & Ruprecht.

Gembris, H. (2005). Die Entwicklung der musikalischen Fähigkeiten. In: H. de la Motte-Haber & G. Rötter (Hrsg.): *Handbuch der Systematischen Musikwissenschaft,* Band 3, 395–456, Laaber: Laaber-Verlag.

Gibson, J. J. (1979). *The ecological approach to visual perception.* Boston: Houghton Mifflin.

Grossmann, K. E. (1997). Bindungserinnerungen und adaptive Perspektiven. In G. Lüer & U. Lass (Hrsg.), *Erinnern und Behalten. Wege zur Erforschung des menschlichen Gedächtnisses,* 321–337. Göttingen: Vandenhoeck & Ruprecht.

Grossmann, K., & Grossmann, K. E. (2004). *Bindungen – das Gefüge psychischer Sicherheit.* Stuttgart: Klett-Cotta.

Holmes, J. (1996). *Attachment, Intimacy, Autonomy: Using Attachment Theory in Adult Psychotherapy.* Northville, New Jersey: Jason Aronson.

Hüther, G. (2003). *Die Bedeutung emotionaler Sicherheit für die Entwicklung des menschlichen Gehirns.* DVD 437D. Auditorium.

Hüther, G. (2004). Ebenen salutogenetischer Wirkungen von Musik auf das Gehirn. *Musiktherapeutische Umschau,* 25/1, 16–26.

Hüther, G. (2007). *Das Symptombild ADS/ADHS.* Auditorium: DVD GLE07-S1D

Jones, W., Carr, K., & Klein, A. (2008). Absence of Preferential Looking to the Eyes of Approaching Adults Predicts Level of Social Disability in 2-Year-Old Toddlers with Autism Spectrum Disorder. *Arch Gen Psychiatry.* 65 (8), 1–9.

Körber, A. (2009). *Beziehungsqualität in der Musiktherapie mit Psychotherapiepatienten. Vergleichende Untersuchung interpersonalen Verhaltens (EBQ, OPD-2, IIP).* VDM Verlag Dr. Müller.

Main, M., Kaplan, N., & Cassidy, J. (1985). Security in infancy, childhood and adulthood: A move to the level of representation. In: I. Bretherton & E. Waters (Eds.), *Growing points of attachment theory and research. Monographs of the Society for Research in child Development,* 50 (1–2, Serial No. 2009, 66–104).

Mangold, P. (2010). *INTERACT Quick Start Manual V2.4.* Mangold International www. mangold-international.com

Meltzoff, A. N., & Moore, (1977). *Imitation of facial gestures and manual gestures by human neonates. Science,* 198, 75–78.

Meltzoff, A. N. (1988) Infant Imitation and Memory: Nine-Month-Olds in Immediate and Deferred Tests. *Child Development,* 1988, 59, 217–225.

Mössler, K., Gold, C., Aßmus, J., Schumacher, K., Calvet, C., Reimer, S., Iversen, G., & Schmid, W. (2017). The therapeutic relationship as predictor of change in music therapy with young children with autism spectrum disorder. J Autism Dev Disord. https://doi.org/10.1007/s10803-017-3306-y.

Moore, C. & Dunham, P. (1995). *Joint attention: Its origin and role in development.* Hillsdale, NJ: Erlbaum.

Muthesius, D., Sonntag, J., Warme, B., & Falk, M. (2010). *Musik Demenz Begegnung: Musiktherapie für Menschen mit Demenz.* Frankfurt a. M.: Mabuse-Verlag.

OPD Task Force (Eds.) (2008): *Operationalized Psychodynamic Diagnosis OPD-2.* Göttingen, Hogrefe & Huber Publishers.

Papoušek, M. (1994). *Vom ersten Schrei zum ersten Wort. Anfänge der Sprachentwicklung in der vorsprachlichen Kommunikation.* Bern, Göttingen: Hans Huber.

Papoušek, M. (2001). *Intuitive elterliche Kompetenzen.* Frühe Kindheit 4, 1, 4–10.

Papoušek, M., Schieche, M., & Wurmser, H. (2004). *Regulationsstörungen der frühen Kindheit. Frühe Risiken und Hilfen im Entwicklungskontext der Eltern-Kind-Beziehungen.* Bern: Hans Huber.

Piaget, J. (1952). *The Origins of Intelligence in Children.* New York: International University Press.

Piaget, J. (1954). *The construction of reality in the child.* New York: Basic Books.

Rauh, H., & Ziegenhain, U. (1994). Nonverbale Kommunikation von Befindlichkeit bei Kleinkindern. In: K.-F. Wessel, & F. Naumann (Hrsg.). Kommunikation und Humanontogenese, 6, 172–218. Bielefeld, Kleine.

Rauh, H., Arens, C., & Calvet-Kruppa, C. (1999). Vulnerabiltät und Resilienz bei Kleinkindern mit geistiger Behinderung. In: G. Opp, M. Fingerle, & A. Freytag (Hrsg.). *Was Kinder stärkt. Erziehung zwischen Risiko und Resilienz*, 101–123. München, Reinhardt.

Rauh, H., & Calvet, C. (2004). Ist Bindungssicherheit entwicklungsfördernd für Kinder mit Down-Syndrom? In: *Kindheit und Entwicklung*, 13, 217–225.

Reimer, S. (2004). Der kurzzeitige Wechsel von Beziehungsqualitäten in der Musiktherapie. *Musiktherapeutische Umschau* 25/2, 135–143.

Reimer, S. (2010). Das EBQ-Instrument in der Arbeit mit schwerst-mehrfachbehinderten Erwachsenen. In: K. Schumacher (Hrsg.). *20 Jahre Studiengang Musiktherapie an der UdK Berlin/AlumniTage 2008.* Musiktherapiezentrum; ZIW, UdK Berlin

Reimer, S. (2016). *Affektregulation in der Musiktherapie mit Menschen mit schwerster Mehrfachbehinderung.* zeitpunkt musik. Wiesbaden: Reichert-Verlag.

Rizzolatti, G., & Sinigaglia, C. (2008). *Mirrors in The Brain: How Our Minds Share Actions and Emotions. New York: Oxford University Press.*

Salmon, S., & Kallos, C. (2010). *„Zwischen Freiraum und Ritual". Ausdrucksmöglichkeiten mit Musik und Bewegung für Menschen mit Behinderung.* Universität Mozarteum Salzburg.

Schmidt J. C., & Schuster, L. (Hrsg.) (2003). *Der entthronte Mensch? Anfragen der Neurowissenschaften an unser Menschenbild.* Paderborn: Mentis-Verlag.

Schumacher, K. (1999). *Musiktherapie und Säuglingsforschung.* Zusammenspiel. Einschätzung der Beziehungsqualität am Beispiel des instrumentalen Ausdrucks eines autistischen Kindes. Frankfurt/M.: Peter Lang.

Schumacher, K. (2009). Autismus. In: H. H. Decker-Voigt (Hg.): *Lexikon Musiktherapie*, 67–73. Göttingen: Hogrefe.

Schumacher, K. (2009). Frühe Mutter – Kindspiele. In: H. H. Decker-Voigt (Hg.): *Lexikon Musiktherapie*, 139–140. Göttingen: Hogrefe.

Schumacher, K. (2014): Music Therapy for pervasive developmental disorders, especially autism - A Case study with theoretical basis and evaluation. In: Jos de Backer, & J. Sutton, *The Music in Music Therapy*. Psychodynamic Music Therapy in Europe: Clinical, Theoretical and Research Approaches, 109–125. London: Kingsley.

Schumacher, K. (2017). *Musiktherapie bei Kindern mit Autismus. Musik-, Bewegungs- und Sprachspiele zur Behandlung gestörter Körper- und Sinneswahrnehmung*. Wiesbaden: Reichert (in press).

Schumacher, K., & Calvet-Kruppa, C. (2001). Die Relevanz entwicklungs-psychologischer Erkenntnisse für die Musiktherapie. In: H.-H. Decker-Voigt (Hrsg.). Schulen der Musiktherapie, 102–124. München: Reinhardt.

Schumacher, K., Calvet, C., & Stallmann, M. (2005). „Zwischenmenschliche Beziehungsfähigkeit" - Ergebnisse der Reliabilitätsprüfung eines neu entwickelten Instrumentes zum Wirkungsnachweis der Musiktherapie. In: Müller-Oursin, B. (Hrsg.): *Ich wachse, wenn ich Musik mache. Musiktherapie mit chronisch kranken und von Behinderung bedrohten Kindern*. Wiesbaden: Reichert.

Schumacher, K., & Calvet-Kruppa, C. (2005). „Untersteh' Dich!" - Musiktherapie bei Kindern mit autistischem Syndrom. In: C. Plahl, H. Koch-Temming: *Musiktherapie für Kinder. Grundlagen, Methoden, Praxisfelder*, 276–284. Bern: Hans Huber.

Schumacher, K., & Calvet, C. (2007). The "AQR-Instrument"– an observation instrument to assess the quality of relationship. In T. Wosch/T. Wigram: *Microanalysis in Music Therapy – Methods, Techniques and Application for Clinicians, Researchers, Educators and Students*. London: Kingsley.

Schumacher, K., & Calvet, C. (2008). *Synchronisation/Synchronization*- Musiktherapie bei Kindern mit Autismus/Music Therapy with Children on the Autistic Spectrum. Unter Mitarbeit von Manfred Hüneke und Petra Kugel. Booklet mit DVD-Box, Göttingen: Vandenhoeck & Ruprecht.

Spangler, G., & Zimmermann, P. (1999). *Die Bindungstheorie: Grundlagen, Forschung und Anwendung*. Stuttgart: Klett-Cotta.

Spitz, R. (1965). *The First Year of Life. A Psychoanalytic Study of Normal and Deviant Development of Object Relations*. New York: International Universities Press.

Sroufe, L. A. (1997). *Emotional Development: The Organization of Emotional Life in the Early Years*. Cambridge: University Press.

Stern, D. (2000). *The Interpersonal World of the Infant*. New York: Basic Books.

Stern, D. (1985). *The Interpersonal World of the Infant*. New York: Basic Books.

Striano, T., & Rochat, P. (2000). Emergence of Selective Social Referencing in Infancy. *Infancy*, 1 (2), 253–264.

Tomasello, M. (1993). On the interpersonal origins of self-concept. In U. Neisser, *The perceived self. Ecological and interpersonal sources of self-knowledge*, 174–185. Cambridge: University Press.

Trevarthen, C. (1993). The self-born in intersubjectivity: The psychology of an infant communicating. In U. Neisser, *The perceived self. Ecological and interpersonal sources of self-knowledge*, 121–173. Cambridge: University Press.

Trevarthen, C. (1998). The concept and foundations of infant intersubjectivity. In: S. Braten (ed.), *Intersubjective communication and emotion in early ontogeny*, 15–46. Cambridge: University Press.

Ziegenhain, U. (2001). Sichere mentale Bindungsmodelle. In: G. Gloger-Tippelt (Hrsg.), *Bindung im Erwachsenenalter*, 154–173. Bern: Hans Huber.

forum zeitpunkt · zeitpunkt musik

Musiktherapie bei Kindern mit Autismus

Musik-, Bewegungs- und Sprachspiele
zur Behandlung gestörter Sinnes- und
Körperwahrnehmung
(mit DVD zum EBQ-Instrument)

Von Karin Schumacher

2017. 8°. 168 S., 3 s/w-Abb., kart., inkl. DVD
(978-3-95490-229-3)

Dieses Buch ist aus der Praxis und für die Praxis geschrieben. Tiefgreifend entwicklungsgestörte Kinder, die mit „Autismus" diagnostiziert wurden, zeigen eine Kontaktstörung nicht nur zu anderen Menschen, sondern auch zu sich selbst. Wahrnehmung und Erleben scheinen nicht selbstverständlich verbunden, die Sinneseindrücke werden vermutlich nicht verlässlich und damit sinngebend verarbeitet. Symptome wie stereotypes Verhalten und Spielunfähigkeit, sowie Sprachlosigkeit bzw. Sprachstörungen sind die Folge. Das Thema „Autismus-Spektrum-Störung" wird zwar in der Fachwelt ausgiebig behandelt, es überwiegen jedoch verhaltensmodifizierende Therapien, die eine Integration in die soziale Welt und ein möglichst selbständiges Leben zum Ziel haben. Neben diesen zweifellos wichtigen Zielen ist aber die Behandlung des Störungsbildes selbst ein anderer Ansatz. In diesem Buch wird ein Therapieverlauf dargestellt, der die eigentliche sozio-emotionale Störung behandelt, die vermutlich auf einer Wahrnehmungsverarbeitungs- und Körpergefühlstörung beruht. Die Kinder, um die es hier geht, sind auch mental eingeschränkt und haben meist keine Sprache entwickelt. Das Medium Musik bietet eine Mitteilungsmöglichkeit, die ihre sozio-emotionale Isolation aufhebt und das Leid dieser Ausdrucksnot mildert. Die Filmausschnitte auf der beigefügten DVD zeigen die Entwicklung des Jungen Max. Ganz vom Kind aus entwickelte Musik-, Bewegungs- und Sprachspiele zeigen, dass ohne die Aufforderung, etwas mit- oder nachmachen zu müssen, Emotionen als Motor jeglicher Entwicklung geweckt werden können. Körperliche, instrumentale sowie stimmlich-vorsprachliche Äußerungen als Voraussetzung für eine kommunikative Sprache werden evoziert und führen spielerisch zur zwischenmenschlichen Verständigung. Die hier genau beschriebenen musiktherapeutischen Interventionen bei tiefgreifend entwicklungsgestörten Kindern mit Autismus zeigen, wie lebendig und entwicklungsfähig diese Kinder sind. Neurobiologische Forschungsergebnisse bestätigen die Notwendigkeit, Wahrnehmung, Erleben, Handlung und Sprache in Verbindung zu bringen. Die Analyse des videographierten Therapieverlaufs mit Hilfe des sogenannten „EBQ-Instrumentes" stellt die Entwicklung des Kindes in der Musiktherapie dar.

forum zeitpunkt · zeitpunkt musik

Spielräume der Musiktherapie

Hg. von Rosemarie Tüpker

2019. 8°. 208 S., 17 s/w-Abb., kart.

(978-3-95490-392-4)

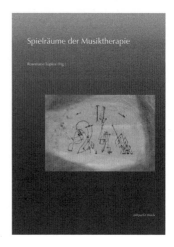

Das Buch handelt von dem Spielraum, den Musiktherapie schaffen kann, indem sie sich beteiligt an der Behandlung seelischen Leids, an der Bearbeitung gesellschaftlicher Konflikte und Notlagen und an der Gestaltung des Miteinanders in Krisen, Krankheiten und schwer zu tragenden Erfahrungen. Diese durchgehende Thematik war auch der Schwerpunkt der Abschiedstagung für Rosemarie Tüpker, die von 1990 bis 2017 die Studiengänge Musiktherapie an der Universität Münster leitete. Das Thema wird von den Beitragenden aus unterschiedlichen Perspektiven und anhand verschiedener relevanter Praxisfelder erörtert, in der Einzelarbeit wie in der Gruppentherapie, im klinischen und außerklinischen Bereich, mit aktiven und rezeptiven Methoden. Im einleitenden Beitrag diskutiert Rosemarie Tüpker das Schaffen und Bewahren von Spielräumen als Behandlungsauftrag der Künstlerischen Therapien. Ein erster Teil des Buches ist mit den Beiträgen von Sandra Lutz Hochreutener, Bernd Reichert, Erika Menebröcker und Anne-Katrin Jordan der Musiktherapie mit Kindern und Jugendlichen gewidmet, bei denen es oft in einem doppelten Sinne um das Spielen geht. Oliver Pauls Beitrag befasst sich mit der Tragik des verloren gegangenen Spielraumes bei Kindern mit Behinderungen. Für die Musiktherapie mit Erwachsenen stehen die methodisch unterschiedlichen Beiträge aus der Psychosomatik von Susanne Bauer, Katharina Nowack und Ruth Liesert sowie aus dem Akutbereich der Psychiatrie von Eva Terbuyken-Röhm. Im Übergang zum außerklinischen Bereich berichtet Sabine Rachl von ihrer Arbeit mit Sterbenden und Heike Plitt zeigt Möglichkeiten einer musiktherapeutischen Arbeit mit Paaren auf. Übergreifende musiktherapeutische Themen finden sich im letzten Teil des Buches mit dem Beitrag zum Spielraum der Stimme durch Oliver Schöndube, der Bedeutung der Intention durch Thomas Adam, mit Reflexionen zum verschlossenen Spielraum (Martin Lenz) und zum Warten (Barbara Keller). Ein Rückblick über die Studiengänge Musiktherapie an der Universität Münster von 1987 bis 2017 beschließt den Band.

forum zeitpunkt · zeitpunkt musik

„… da bewegt sich was …" –
Intermediale Musiktherapie in sozialen Berufen

Von Hans-Helmut Decker-Voigt und mit einem
Praxisteil von Constanze Rüdenauer-Speck

Hg. von Kurt Brust -
Institut für soziale Berufe Ravensburg

2018. 8°. 295 S., 7 s/w- und 125 Farbabb., kart.
(978-3-95490-383-2)

Jede Gestaltung mit künstlerischen Medien „bewegt" und ändert damit die Psychodynamik der einzelnen KlientInnen/PatientInnen bzw. die Dynamik einer Gruppe. Dieses Buch führt ein in die Arbeit mit intermedialen Verfahrensschritten: Die Verbindung einzelner künstlerischer Medien wie Musik, Bewegung/Tanz, Sprache, Malen/Bildnerisches Gestalten, digitale Instrumente und der Natur als Co-Therapeutin. Die jahrelange Zusammenarbeit von Paolo J. Knill (Ausdruckstherapie) und Hans-Helmut Decker-Voigt (Musik- und Medientherapie) veranlasst den Herausgeber anzuregen, diese Verfahren für die sozialen Berufe unter Einbeziehung der neuen digitalen Medien sowie der uralten der Natur für soziale Berufe aufzubereiten. Der Praxisteil von Constanze Rüdenauer-Speck lädt ein zu Spielprozessen „von einem Medium zum anderen", die zusammen mit dem Grundlagenteil sowohl therapeutisch als auch sozial- und heilpädagogisch aufbereitet werden können.

forum zeitpunkt · zeitpunkt musik

Rhythmik – Musik und Bewegung im Dialog

Versuch einer Klärung

Von Brigitte Steinmann

2018. 8°. 138 S., 1 s/w-Abb., kart.
(978-3-95490-358-0)

Rhythmik versteht sich als Handlungsfeld in Kunst und Pädagogik, in dem dialogisch und fächer-übergreifend mit Musik und Bewegung agiert wird. Obwohl Kenner die Rhythmik zu schätzen wissen, fehlt es dem Fach an sich und dem Studiengang an Musikhochschulen im Speziellen an Anerkennung. Fehlendes Verständnis für die inhaltlichen, historischen und interdisziplinären Zu-sammenhänge führten und führen immer wieder zu falschen Auslegungen. Ursachen davon wird in dem vorliegenden Band nachgegangen, dem Leser werden Details erklärt und begründet, auf offensichtliche Unklarheiten wird eingegangen. Dass der Bewegung eine besondere Bedeutung in der Musikpädagogik und beim Musizieren sowie in der Wahrnehmung und Gestaltung von Leben zukommt, ist unbestritten. Deshalb ist es gerechtfertigt, einen hohen Anspruch an die Ausbildung und Berufsausübung von Rhythmikern – Künstlern und Pädagogen – zu stellen. Das bedarf der Präzisierung in der Darstellung, in Begrifflichkeiten und im Handeln. Der Versuch einer Klärung ist ein Plädoyer für die Rhythmik und ihre Bewahrung als traditionsreiches, elementares Teilgebiet der Musik und der Musikpädagogik.